PYTHON *For* DATA SCIENCE

THE ULTIMATE COMPREHENSIVE STEP-BY-STEP GUIDE TO THE BASICS OF PYTHON FOR DATA SCIENCE

KEVIN CLARK

TABLE OF CONTENTS

Introduction

Data science is the discipline that combines ideas from Statistics and Computer Science to solve the problem of knowledge discovery in databases. In this partnership, Statistics has the role of providing the tools to describe, analyze, summarize, interpret, and make inferences about the data. In turn, Computer Science is concerned with providing efficient technologies for the storage, access, integration, and transformation of data.

That is, the role of Computer Science is to make feasible the analysis of databases, often complex and voluminous, through statistical processes. Among the different technologies used for scientific computing, Python is undoubtedly one of the most prominent. It is a free programming language, extremely versatile and powerful, which has been widely adopted in projects related to data science, both by industry and the academic community.

This book presents the fundamental concepts and techniques for those who wish to start working with Python for data science. The book covers the computational aspects of data science, which means that its main focus is to teach the reader how to develop programs capable of processing databases of different sizes, formats, and degrees of complexity.

The work is intended for all types of professionals involved with data science: biologists, mathematicians, engineers, chemists, administrators, physicists, statisticians, economists, etc., in short, anyone who wants to learn how to develop their own Python scripts to explore databases related to problems in their area of expertise.

Reiterating: the book is not only intended for people with backgrounds in computing but all human beings interested in Python for data science. It is also important to make it clear that the book does not focus on teaching statistics, machine learning, or data mining. In fact, what we intend is to teach the reader to program in the Python language, enabling him, in the future, to develop any type of script in this language, including programs that can analyze large databases through statistical methods or using algorithms for machine learning and data mining. In short, what we want is to make the reader a top-notch pythonist1!

No prerequisites are required for reading the book, although knowledge of some programming language - such as R, MATLAB, C, or even Excel's macro programming - certainly helps speed up the learning process. The book is divided into five very broad chapters. The first three cover the language's "rice and beans," that is, the least you need to know to start developing any kind of Python application. The following chapters deal with themes that are more directly related to data science.

- Chapter 1 - Pleasure to meet you, Python Language. It aims to present the Python environment and teach the reader how to create their first programs.

- Chapter 2 - Creating and Using Functions. Data analysis is always facilitated with the use of functions. In this chapter, you will discover how to use the basic mathematical and statistical functions of Python and also learn how to create your own reusable functions and modules.

- Chapter 3 - Native Data Structures. Data structures are used by programming languages to organize related data sets in memory to make their manipulation simpler and more efficient. This chapter presents the four native data structures of Python: lists, tuples, sets, and dictionaries.

- Chapter 4 - Strings and Databases in Text Format. Before statistical techniques can analyze data, it needs to be loaded into the Python environment. This chapter presents the basic techniques for importing text databases structured in different ways: CSV, JSON, column separated file, etc. In addition, the chapter presents the numerous word processing tools offered by Python, from simple string functions to regular expressions.

3

- Chapter 5 - SQL Database and Language. The main purpose of this chapter is to teach you how to query, combine, and explore tables stored in relational databases using the SQL language. Although SQL is more than 35 years old, it remains very relevant and is currently considered one of the key technologies in the area of data science.

Much of the text presented in this book refers to Python code (small programs that demonstrate the concepts presented) and the results produced by the code (usually in the form of printed output on the screen). The following typographical conventions have been adopted:

- Constant font width: Used in the listings of Python programs and in the presentation of the contents of structured databases in text files.

- Bold font with constant width: Used to represent the names of reserved words, functions, and some operators of the Python language. This convention is adopted both in the lists of programs and in the texts explaining their operation.

- "Word in double quotation marks": Used in explanatory texts to highlight names of variables, files, and other objects (DataFrames, arrays, database tables, etc.).

Chapter One

Very Pleasure, Python Language

This chapter aims to make a presentation of the Python environment, as well as teach you how to write your first programs in the language. We begin by explaining what Python is and discussing why this technology has become fundamental to data science. We then present the step-by-step roadmap for installing, configuring, and using WinPython, one of the simplest environments for scientific programming in Python.

From there, the chapter to addresses programming itself through a sequence of lessons that aims to introduce the basic features of the Python language: variables, arithmetic operators, input and output, deviation structures, repetition structures, and code blocks. Closing the chapter, we present a brief comparison between Python and R, the two technologies that currently compete for the most important programming language post for data science.

What is Python?

Python is a general-purpose programming language, which means that it can be used in many different types of projects, ranging from web applications to artificial intelligence systems. The language was created in 1991, with the main philosophy of prioritizing the construction of simple and readable programs (what pythonists call "beautiful" programs) over the construction of programs that, although fast, are complicated and difficult to read (the so-called "ugly" programs).

Over the next ten years, language has achieved great popularity in both academic and corporate environments. This motivated the emergence of the Python Software Foundation in 2001, an independent, non-profit institution that became responsible for developing new versions of the language (at the time of writing this book, the most recent version was 3.7.2).

In recent years, Python has consolidated itself as one of the most widespread technologies in the field of data science, although it was not originally designed for this purpose. This achievement was not only because the language facilitates the creation of "cute little face" programs! In fact, the success of Python for data science is related to other of its characteristics, as shown below:

- Since Python is an interpreted language, beginners can learn some commands and start doing cool things (e.g., applying mathematical functions and statistics to datasets) almost immediately, without encountering problems related to the code building. And to make things even better, the Python interpreter can be used interactively, where every command you type is immediately translated and executed. This offers programmers an agile and simple way to examine in real-time the intermediate results obtained in any step of a data analysis process.

- Python is an open-source language. On the Python Software Foundation2 website, it is possible to download for free the file that installs the Python interpreter and its standard library. Together, these components form the "heart" of the Python environment, offering a rich set of data structures (such as lists and dictionaries). They also offer hundreds of modules aimed at the execution of the most diverse types of tasks, from the use of mathematical and statistical functions to the processing of text files in different formats (CSV, JSON, etc.).

- The Python language can be easily extended by incorporating other packages. There are currently thousands of packages available in the Python Package Index (PyPI) central repository. Many, many of them are data science-oriented, such as 'NumPy' (manipulation of vectors and matrices), 'SciPy' (integration and numerical calculation), 'pandas' (manipulation of DataFrames), 'Matplotlib' (graph generation) and 'Scikit-learn' (algorithms for data mining and machine learning).

- Finally, Python is a multiparadigm language that allows both procedural and object-oriented program design. The procedural paradigm is simpler but perfect for developing data science scripts. This is because it does not require the programmer to master certain concepts that are very specific to the area of software engineering3 (such as defining classes and methods and developing detailed routines for exception handling). This characteristic of the procedural style is very important in the area of data science, where programmers are often not people with backgrounds in computing. They are also biologists, statisticians, chemists, etc., who just want to create a very lean and direct program to explore a particular database.

On the other hand, the object-oriented paradigm is sophisticated and complex, being, however, the most indicated for the construction of applications and information systems. In programs of this type, the developer needs to worry about several issues that are not usually parts of the world of data analysis, such as session management, menu creation, and access control, to name but a few. It is precisely in the object-oriented paradigm that the most suitable tools to deal with these problems are offered.

Very Pleasure, Python Language

- Python is a general-purpose, interpreted, interactive, free, and multiparadigm language.

- It is an extremely versatile and powerful language that has a large number of packages for data science (statistical packages, mathematics, data mining, artificial intelligence, machine learning, numerical calculation, etc.). Therefore, it has been adopted by an increasing number of companies.

- Despite the design of the two little snakes on the logo, the name "Python" does not represent a tribute to the python snake4. In fact, it is a reference5 to the English comedy group Monty Python6.

Python Distributions

Being an "all-round language" (general purpose), free and very popular, Python has an impressive ecosystem of packages that have already reached tens of thousands! They are destined to the most different types of problems: some service for the creation of games, many of them are for the development of Web applications, some others for the development of embedded systems, there is a good number that offers algorithms for machine learning, and so on. There's even no way to try to make a complete list because the number of distinct problem categories covered by Python packages is really huge!

This situation motivated the emergence of different distributions of the Python environment. A distribution (or distro) is nothing more than a collection of selected packages and applications, which are brought together in a single installer file because they are considered to be "most suitable" for a particular purpose. The table below shows two examples of well-known distributions, CPython and WinPython.

CPython Distribution	WinPython Distribution
Python interpreter	Python interpreter
Standard Library	Standard Library
Basic utilities (IPython, pip, etc.)	Basic utilities (IPython, pip, etc.)
	NumPy
	pandas
	Matplotlib

	Scikit-learn
	i SciPy '
	Spyder
	'Jupyter Notebook'
	...

CPython is the official Python distribution, managed by the Python Software Foundation, whose installer file for different platforms - Windows, Mac, Linux - can be obtained from https://www.python.org/https://www.python.org/. This is the reference version of Python, which comes basically with the double interpreter + standard library and a small set of basic utilities. You could say it's a "neutral" distribution. This distribution installs no data science packages. However, CPython provides an application called "pip" that makes it possible to install later any package that is part of the PyPI repository. Information on CPython and pip is given in Annex B.

In turn, the WinPython distribution was created specifically for the Windows environment, is intended for those who wish to work with Python for data science. Its most attractive feature is the fact that it does not need to be installed; in fact, just unzip the installer file into some folder on your computer and, that's it, you can start programming now! WinPython already comes with over 300 packages and applications for data science: 'NumPy,' 'pandas,' 'Matplotlib,' 'Spyder,' etc., which can be used immediately, without the need for any additional installation steps.

Due to the simplicity of its configuration process and the fact that it is a data science-driven distribution, we decided to adopt WinPython as the default Python environment for executing the examples presented in this book. In the next lesson, you will learn the steps necessary to download and install it. However, it is important to note that this is not the best Python distribution; it is just a good starting point for those who are starting to work with this language.

Another problem with WinPython is that it is not available for Linux and Mac. If you use these operating systems, an interesting alternative is to use the Anaconda distribution (https://www.anaconda.com/download/), which is also focused on data science, being even more comprehensive (comes as more than 700 packages). Another option is to build an environment from the CPython distribution, but also installing the main data science packages using pip.

Python Versions - Python 2 versus Python 3

- Python versions are numbered as x.y.z (e.g., Python 3.7.2). In this scheme of numbering, we have to:

  - "x" represents the major version number, incremented only when it occurs

  - extremely significant changes in language.

  - "y" is the secondary number, incremented when less significant changes occur.

  - Z "z" is micro-level, usually incremented when bugfixes (occur problems).

- In 2008, the Python Software Foundation decided to make a radical change in the Python 3 release. This new series is not completely compatible with the Python 2 series, which means that many programs implemented in Python version 2.a.b may not run on Python version 3.c.d.

- Therefore, when you download distribution, you should always choose the installer Python 3 is no longer worth working with Python 2 as this version is considered obsolete and should be discontinued on 1st January 2020 (at least this is Python Software Foundation prediction).

WinPython Installation

The following are the steps for installing WinPython on a machine with Windows 7 or higher operating system.

Installation on 64-bit Windows Systems

- Access the WinPython repository: https://sourceforge.net/projects/winpython/ Shown in the below figure.

- Download the installation file (64-bit version): If your operating system is 64-bit, click the Download button. After a few seconds, the installation file will start downloading automatically. At the time of writing this book, the last stable version of the software was number 3.6.7 (so the file was named "WinPython64-3.6.7.0Qt5.exe"). The download process will take some time to complete, as the installation file has more than 460MB.

- Installing WinPython: At the end of the download, run the downloaded file to start the WinPython installation process on your machine. The installation is a bit time-consuming, however, very simple, in that good old "Next Next Next" scheme. It is worth paying attention to the second screen (the screen that appears right after the first "Next," shown in the next Figure) because at this moment, and you can specify the folder destination of the

14

installation. In the installation I did on my machine, I chose to change the initial suggestion to a simpler path ("C:\WPY3670"). With regard to disk space, WinPython is a bit greedy, requiring more than 2GB of free space on your hard drive.

Installation on 32-bit Windows Systems

- Navigating to the "Files" folder: installing WinPython on 32-bit systems starts a little bit differently, because, first of all, you need to navigate to the page that contains the different versions of the distribution. So, after accessing the WinPython repository (https://sourceforge.net/projects/winpython/), you should click on Files, as highlighted in the next Figure (not to click on the Download button, but on Files!!!!).

- Download the installation file (32-bit version): the screen of Figure 5 will appear, where the various versions of the distribution are listed, each with its link for download. Note that there is a green button stating that the latest stable version is "WinPython64-3.6.7" (the button that says "Download Latest Version"). Do not click this button, because it will result in the download of the 64-bit version. Instead, click on the WinPython_3.6 link (highlighted in Figure below) to access the 32-bit version of

WinPython 3.6.7. In the window that will open, then click on 3.6.7.0. Finally, click on the file "WinPython32-3.6.7.0Qt5.exe". Okay, okay, okay, okay, okay. The file will start downloading.

- o **Important:** the great mallet in the 32-bit installation is first to identify which is the number of the last stable version (this is done by observing the green button, where is written "Download Latest Version"). Once identified, you must click on the link that has the version number to access the 32-bit installer.

- Installing WinPython: Once the download is complete, just follow the guidelines in item 3.1.3 to install WinPython.

Using WinPython in Interactive Mode

Python programs can be run in two modes: normal and interactive. In normal mode, the program is first typed in completely, then saved, and then run "cable to cable" (i.e., completely, without pauses) by the Python interpreter. Conversely, when we're working in interactive mode, Python interprets and executes command by command as they are typed. Using WinPython in normal mode will be handled in the next lesson. In this one, we present the recipe to work with WinPython in interactive mode. Just follow the steps below:

- Starting QtConsole: Open Windows Explorer and access the folder you chose to unzip WinPython. Then double-click on the "IPython Qt Console.exe" program. This is a slightly more "nice" version of IPython, Python's best known interactive terminal.

- Typing your first command: we can simply test WinPython by typing $1 + 1$. You will type in the part of the screen that displays "In [1]:" (called an input prompt). Just do as indicated below:

```
In [1]: 1 + 1
Out [1]: 2
In [2]:
```

  - The value 2 will be returned after the display "Out [1]:" and a new prompt for data entry will appear just below it, this time represented by "In [2]:". The interactive mode always works this way: we type a command line, and Python processes it immediately, and then it's ready, so we can type another command.

- Typing one more command: this time, we can risk something more classic: the command to write "Hello Python!" on the screen. Just use the print() function and write the message in single quotes, in parentheses:

```
In [1]: 1 + 1
Out [1]: 2
```

```
In [2]: print('Olá Python!')
Olá Python!
In [3]:
```

- Ending the conversation with Python: when you want to close the QtConsole type quit() or simply close the application window.

```
In [1]: 1 + 1
Oct [1]: 2
In [2]: print ('Hello Python!')
Hello Python!
In [3]: quit ()
```

Using WinPython in Normal Mode

Integrated Development Environment (IDE) is a jargon used in the area of software engineering to label applications intended to serve as an environment for the creation, debugging, and execution of programs in a given language. The great advantage of using an IDE is that this type of software usually offers a series of features capable of increasing the efficiency of the programming process. Some examples:

- **Autocomplete** - allows a command to be automatically completed during typing

- Inline help - displays a help text about a reserved word when the mouse is placed over it

- Automatic program formatting - performs automatic alignment of commands that are placed between the beginning and the end of an instruction block.

Just to present some well-known examples of IDEs, we can mention the Eclipse application, for the creation of programs in the Java language, and RStudio, for the development in R.

There are many, many IDEs available for Python, such as PyCharm, Rodeo, Jupyter Notebook, and Spyder. On the Internet, you will find good articles that discuss the advantages and disadvantages of each of them. In this book, we will adopt Spyder since this IDE is optimized for data science projects, besides being very intuitive and allowing the use of Python in both normal and interactive modes. The disadvantage of this software is that it is a bit heavy, requiring a considerable amount of memory to run. However, if you have a machine with reasonable processing power, it is worth working with this IDE. The following example shows the step by step for you to use Python in normal mode through Spyder.

- Start the Spyder IDE: open Windows Explorer and access the folder you chose to unzip WinPython, then double-click on the "Spyder.exe" program. After a while, the main Spyder screen will be displayed.

- Enter the program: type, in the code editor area, a program with a single line: print('Hello Python!'). Don't be alarmed that Spyder already automatically places some header lines (lines between #-*- coding: utf-8 -*- e """). Just type your program just below them, from line 8.

- Saving the program: the program is entered but has not yet been saved. There are two ways to do this: by using the File > Save menu or by typing CTRL + S. Then choose a folder and give the program a name. The folder chosen was "C:\CursoPython" and the program name "OlaPython.py." The ".py" extension was used because it is the standard Python extension (just like ".java" is used by Java programs, ".c" by C programs, etc.).

- Executing the program: there are a few different ways:

  o Select the menu option Run > Run; or

  o Click the "execute file" button (highlighted in Figure 9);

  o Simply press F5.

- Verify the results: the program output (execution result) will be displayed in the IPython Console, which consists of the area located in the lower right corner of the screen (indicated by "3-Results" in Figure 9). This console also allows you to use Python in interactive mode.

Now that you have installed WinPython and know how to create and run programs both in interactive and normal mode take a deep breath and get ready! The next lessons in this book have been carefully prepared for you to become a true pythonist!

Python Programming: Getting Started

Variables and Types

A variable can be understood as the name of a place where any numeric or non-numeric value can be placed. The following code exemplifies the use of variables in Python programs and presents the types of basic data offered by the language. In this example, as well as in the others presented throughout the book, the program code is shown first, and the result of the execution is shown below. The result will always be listed in red letters, after the "Output [n]:" prompt, where n is the number of the example program.

Program 1 - Use of Variables to Store a Person's Information

```
#P001: variables and types; functions type() and
print()

#PART 1: variable declaration

first name = 'Jane' last name = 'Austen' age = 41

note = 9.9 approved = True
```

#PART 2: Printing the content of variables and their types

print(first name, last name, age, grade, approved)

print(type(first)) print(type(last)) print(type(age)) print(type(note)) print(type(approved))

#PART 3: changing the value and type of the "note" variable

note = 'A'

print('changed the value and type of "note" to: ', note, ',', type(note))

Output [1]:

```
Jane Austen 41 9.9 True
<class 'str'>
<class 'str'>
<class 'int'>
<class 'float'>
<bool' class.
```

I've changed the value and type of "grade" to..: A, <class 'str'>

To begin with, it is important to mention that this is a typical example of a procedural program whose execution flow (order in which the Python interpreter executes commands) is from top to bottom in sequence.

The program was divided into three parts. Let's get to the explanations on each one:

- In PART 1, the declarations of the variables "first name", "last name", "age", "grade" and "approved" are provided. These variables are declared, respectively, with values of type str (string abbreviation, i.e., alphanumeric, both "first name" and "last name"), int (integer values), float (real values) and bool (logical values: True or False). These are Python's four types of primitive data. The name "primitive" refers to the fact that these are the simplest types of values with which language works.

  - The assignment operator, represented by the symbol "=," is used to assign a value (right side of the equation) to a variable (left side). For example: note = 9.9. The associated value need not always be fixed; it can also be another variable (for example, a = b) or an expression (square_perimeter = 4 * side).

  - In Python, the declaration of variables can be made in any line of the program. The type of variable will be automatically determined according to the value assigned to it and may change during the execution of the program if the value of the variable is changed.

- o String values can be defined in single quotation marks (first name = 'Jane') or double quotation marks (last name = 'Austen').

- PART 2 covers the use of print(), the standard function for data output. To print several variables, simply separate them by commas. Note that values of any kind can be printed with this command. Also, in this part, we use the type() function, a very useful function that returns the type of data stored in a variable.

- In PART 3, it is shown how a variable can have not only its value, but also its type modified during the execution flow. In this code snippet, the "note" value is changed from 9.9 (float type) to 'A' (str type).

Comments

Comments are texts or phrases defined using the # symbol. In the previous program, note that the first line contains a text with comments:

#P001: variables and types; functions type() and print()

The Python interpreter ignores comments at the time the program is processed. They are only for documentation, that is, to be read by humans who are analyzing or changing the program. In practice, they are very useful for facilitating the understanding of a complex routine (set of instructions).

Variable Names

- As introduced in the first section, Python is a language that prioritizes code readability. For this reason, pythonists are encouraged to choose names that can clearly express the meaning of variables (even if they become large). There is even a style guide called PEP-8, which offers a series of rules that the programmer can apply to make his code more readable. This guide recommends that all variables should have the name specified in lower case and that the underscore (_) character be used to separate compound names. Some examples:

  - age

  - annual_median_income

  - code_occupation

  - products_2019

- Names may contain letters, numbers, and the underscore character; however, they cannot be started by a number. There is a differentiation between upper and lower case letters, which means that if you name a variable as "x," you cannot reference it as "X" (but remember that the recommendation is to use lower case in the names of all variables).

- The name of a variable can also not be the same as a keyword in the Python language, the full list of which is given below:

and	elif	if	or
the	else	import	pass
assert	except	in	raise
break	False	is	return
class	finally	lambda	True
continue	for	None	try
def	from	nonlocal	while
del	overall	not	with
			yield

Expressions

The following program covers basic mathematical operations. The +, -, *, /, and ** operators are used, respectively, to perform addition, subtraction, multiplication, division, and exponentiation. The operator // returns the quotient of an entire room, while % returns the module (remainder). Any operation follows the basic order known as PEMDAS (parentheses, exponentiation, multiplication, division, addition, and subtraction).

Program 2 - Basic Mathematical Operations

```
#P002: Basic math

# Addition, subtraction, multiplication and
division

x=5; y=2

print(x+y, x-y, x*y, x/y)

print(y**x)

#quociente and rest (or module)

quotient = x // y module = x % y

print("The quotient of the division of", x, "by",
y, "is: ", quotient)

print("The division module of", x, "by", y, "is: ",
module) #expression in parentheses

e1 = (1 + 2) * 5**2 / ((5-3) + 1)

print("The value of the expression e1 is: ", e1)

#? the division of two integers always generates
a float

# (even if the division is exact)

a=10; b=5; c=a/b
```

```
print(a, b, c)

print(type(a), type(b), type(c))
```

Output [2]:

```
7 3 10 2.5
32
```

The division quotient of 5 by 2 is 2 The division module of 5 by 2 is: 1

The value of expression e1 is: 25.0 10 5 2.0

<class 'int'> <class 'int'> <class 'float'>32

Two important observations:

- It is possible to write more than one command on a single line by separating them by a semicolon. For example: a=10; b=5; c=a/b. However, according to "good programming practices" (PEP-8), you should avoid producing a line that is longer than 72 characters.

- As shown in the last three lines of the program, in Python 3, the result of splitting two integers will always result in a real (float) value.

Keyboard Data Entry

The Python language has a function called input() that allows data entry via keyboard.

Program 3 - Receives the Name of a Person Via Keyboard

```
#P003: Data entry

name = input("What's your name? \n")

print("Hmmm... so you're the famous " + name)
```

Output [3]:

```
What's your name?
>       John Lennon
```

Hmmm... so you're the famous John Lennon.

Explanation:

- When the input() function is called, the program "stops" and waits for the user to type something. After the user finishes typing and typing Enter, the function will return the value entered via the keyboard as a string. This value can then be stored in a variable (in the example, it was stored in the variable "name").

- In the first line of the program, the strange "\n" sequence was used to force a line break after the question "What's your name?". This sequence is also commonly used within the print() function. In fact, it is widely used in programs written in different programming languages, being entitled "newline format."

- In the second line of the program, the + operator is used to concatenate strings, that is, to join the phrase "Hmm... so you're the famous one" with the value of the variable "name."

- In data science, programs usually receive only files or databases as input and, therefore, the input() function is practically not used.

Conditional Deviation Instructions: if, else, elif

In any data analysis script, situations will always occur in which it will be necessary to analyze conditions in order to, only then, define the behavior of the program. The if and else instructions are those used for this purpose. They're called conditional diversion instructions.

Program 4 - Conditional Deviation With if: - else

In this example, the if-else structure is used to check the age of a person who wants to enter a party (the value is stored in the variable "age") by making a comparison with the integer value 18. If (if) the age is 18 or older, then a message inviting you to enter is displayed on the screen. Otherwise (else), a message informing that the citizen is properly barred is displayed on the screen (it is no use even he argue that he is 17 years and 11 months because "age" is the whole type!!!!). If you have any questions, test the program at different times by modifying the value of the variable "age."

#P004: Conditional deviation with if: - else:

```
age = 17

if (age >= 18) :

print ("Come on in, the party's pumping!")

print("We have a lot of music and special drinks!!!!")

else :

print("You're too young for this club! Only come back when you're 18.")
```

Output [4]:

```
You're too young for this club! Don't
come back until you're 18.
```

Note that the if and else commands end with a colon ":" and that the subordinate lines of each command (also called subordinate code blocks) are indented. In this example, the if has two subordinate commands and the else only one. The following section describes in detail the schema used by Python to define code blocks.

Code Blocks

To start with, a warning: pay attention, a lot of attention, because you will see a very peculiar feature of Python. Unlike any other programming language, code blocks that are subordinated to if, else, and other commands that will still be displayed, as for and while, are defined through the indentation of commands7. While Pascal uses the words begin and end to mark a block and languages like C, Java, and R, use the symbols "{" and "}," Python uses blanks or tabs.

That's right: blanks or tabs. This means that the commands must be aligned in the same way for Python to recognize them as part of a block. The convention is to use four spaces for indentation (this is a further recommendation from PEP-8). However, the language allows any alignment pattern (e.g., a tab, three spaces, etc.), as long as it is repeated for all commands belonging to the same block. To make the concept clear, observe the example below:

Indentation Error:	Correct Indentation:
if (x> 0):	if (x> 0):
a = 1	a = 1

IndentationError: expected an indented block

Beware of Copy and Paste!

- If you try to select and copy program code from this PDF file, realize that they will lose their indentation when pasted to their destination, be that the editor Spyder code or any other location.

- However, don't forget that this book comes with a ZIP archive ("CursoPython.zip"), which contains all the programs and databases presented throughout the chapters (in any case, read the Purpose Section). Just copy and paste the code from the ZIP archive programs, so the indentation will be preserved.

Relational and Logical Operators

The if instruction assesses a condition before making a decision. A condition represents a comparison or set of comparisons that will always result in a logical (boolean) value, i.e., TRUE or FALSE. In the Python language, the operators used in the conditions - called relational operators - are the following:

x	== y	#	*the value of x is*	*equal to that of y?*
x	!= y	#	*the value of x is*	*different from the value of y?*
x	> y	#	*the value of x is*	*bigger than y's?*
x	< y	#	*the value of x is*	*smaller than that of y?*
x	>= y	#	*the value of x is*	*greater than or equal to that of y?*
x	<= y	#	*the value of x is*	*less than or equal to that of y?*

x is y

x is not y

x and y point/not point to the same memory address?
(details in Chapter III)

The logical operators and (e), or (or) and not (not) can be used to join different conditions, thus increasing the complexity of the tests. They work like this:

- and# *the sentence is true if ALL the*

Conditions are true

- or# *the sentence is true if ONE of the*

Conditions are true

- not# inverts the logical value of a # sentence (True → False, False

→ True)

Program 5 - Miscellaneous Examples Involving Relational and Logical Operators

```
#P005: relational and logical operators print('* *
* * part 1 * * * * * ') print(4 * 2 == 8)#True.

print(9 ** 2 == 81)#True.

print(5 + 2 < 7)#False.

print(5 + 2 >= 7)#True. print('Newyork' ==
'Newgersey') #False. print(5 / 2 > 3)#False.

print(7 % 2 != 0)#True.
```

```
print('n*n* * * part 2 * * * * * ') parents =
'Brazil'.

print(parents == 'USA') #True.

print(parents == 'Usa') #False.

media_final = 7.0

if (media_final >= 7.0):

print('with media', media_final, 'you are
approved')

else:

print('failed')


a=10; b=100

if (a >= b):

print('the value of "a" is greater than or equal to
that of "b"')

else:

print('the value of "a" is smaller than that of
"b"')


print('n*n* * * part 3 * * * * * ')
```

```
print((4 * 2 == 8) and (9**2 >= 81))#True.
print((1 + 1 < 3) and (9**2 > 81))#False.
print((1 + 1 < 3) or ('flu' == 'fla')) #True.
```

Output [5]:

```
* * * * part 1 * * * *
* True *
True
False
True
False
False
True
False

* * * * part 2 * * * *
 True
False
```

with an average of 7.0, you are approved

the value of "a" is less than the value of "b."

```
* * * * part 3 * * *
* True *
False
True
```

In situations where more than two logic operators need to be used to assemble a logic test, the order of precedence shown in Table 1 will be adopted.

Operator	Valuation order
not	1
and	2
or	3

The not operator has the highest priority (he is the first to be evaluated), followed by and or, respectively. These rules of precedence can be superimposed through the use of parentheses. To make the concept clear, consider the scenario described below. Suppose you are developing a program to process a product database. On this basis, there are five different product categories: 'A,' 'B,' 'C,' 'D' and 'E.' Imagine that you want to produce a report that will list only products in the categories 'A' and 'B' that cost less than $500.00. In a situation like this, if you mount your diversion structure as shown below, you will end up selecting products that should not belong to the listing:

```
price = 999.99; category = 'B
if category==='B' or category=='A' and
price < 500: print('selected')
else:
print('not selected')
```

Output [1]:

```
Selected
```

Because the and operator takes precedence over the or operator, Python tests the specified condition in bold red first. That is, the test will be interpreted by Python as follows: "select the product if the category is equal to 'A' and the price is less than 500; or if the category is 'B.' For this reason, the program would end up listing all products that have category 'B,' regardless of whether the price is less than 500 or not. Notice now the program correction, where the parentheses are used to change the precedence and thus include in the listing only the correct products:

```
price = 999.99; category = 'B

if (category=='B' or category=='A') and
price < 500:
print('selected')

else:
print('not selected')
```

Output [1]:

```
not selected
```

Elif instruction

In many practical situations, there is a need to evaluate more than two possibilities in a conditional test. In this situation, the tests can be logically grouped using the elif instruction (not "else if" or "elsif," the name of the instruction is "elif"). In Program 6, the if-elif-else structure is used to determine the category of a numerical value (a typical application for this structure in data analysis programs).

Program 6 - Returns the Age Range of a Person According to their Age

```
#P006: if, elif, else
age = 25

if (age < 18): age group = '<18'.
elif (age >= 18 and age < 30): age group
= '18-29
elif (age >= 30 and age < 40): age group
= '30-39
else:
age_range = '>=40'

print('If age is', age, 'then age range
is :', age_range)
```

Output [6]:

```
If the age is 25, then the age group is:
18-29
```

Python does not have a case or switch structure, present in other programming languages. That is: what you would implement with case-switch in another language, you will do with if-elif-else in Python.

Nested Conditionals Instructions

To end the lesson, the following is an example code that contains an if inside an else. To implement such a routine - if inside of else, if inside of if, or anything like that - it is also necessary to make use of indentation.

Program 7 - Data Two Numbers - Checks which is the Greater or if Both are Equal

```
#P007: nested conditional instructions

a=5; b=10

if (a == b):

print("a and b are equal")

else:

if (a > b):

print("a is greater than b")

else:

print("a is smaller than b")
```

Output [7]:

```
a is less than b
```

Here is the summary of the syntax of conditional bypass commands.

- if alone (can have one or more subordinate commands)

  ```
  if <condition>:
  command₁
  ...
  commandₙ
  ```

- if with else (both can have one or more subordinate commands)

  ```
  if <condition>:
  command₁
  ...
  commandₙ
  else :
  command₁
  ...
  commandₙ
  ```

- If + elif + else (each can have one or more subordinate commands)

  ```
  if <condition1>:
  command₁
  ...
  commandₙ
  elif <condition2>:
  command₁
  ...
  commandₙ
  ...
  ```

```
elif <condition>:
command₁
...
commandₙ
else :
command₁
...
commandₙ
```

Repeat Instructions (1): while

A repetition structure (or loop) allows an instruction block to be executed several times until a condition is met. In the Python language, there are two types of repetition structure: while and for.

In Python, the while command works the same way as in other programming languages: while the specified condition value next to the while word is true, the code block subordinate to the command is executed. When it's false, the command is abandoned. If, in the first test, the result is false, the commands are not executed at all. The syntax of the command is shown below.

```
while <condition>:
    command₁
    ...
    commandₙ
```

Program 8 - Table of Equivalence between Degrees Celsius and Degrees Fahrenheit

In this table, -20o C is the initial temperature value and 100o C the end. The scale of the table in degrees Celsius varies from 10 to 10.

> #P008: repetition with the while command (first example)
>
> c = -20
>
> print('* * * * Table of conversion from degrees Celsius to degrees Fahrenheit')
>
> while c <= 100: f=c*1.8 + 32
>
> print(c,'ºC ----> ',f,'ºF') c=c+10
>
>
> print ('END!!!!!')

Output [8]:

* * * Conversion table from degrees Celsius to degrees Fahrenheit

```
-20 ºC ----> -4.0 ºF
-10 ºC ----> 14.0 ºF
0 ºC ----> 32.0 ºF
10 ºC ----> 50.0 ºF
20 ºC ----> 68.0 ºF
30 ºC ----> 86.0 ºF
40 ºC ----> 104.0 ºF
```

```
 50 ºC ----> 122.0 ºF
 60 ºC ----> 140.0 ºF
 70 ºC ----> 158.0 ºF
 80 ºC ----> 176.0 ºF
 90 ºC ----> 194.0 ºF
100 ºC ----> 212.0 ºF
END!!!!
```

Variable "c" is called a control variable because it is used to control the loop, that is, to keep it running during the number of repetitions desired. It is initialized outside the loop and is updated inside the loop, as it should happen whenever we use the while. Each repetition performed within a loop is called an iteration. Thus, the program above performed 13 iterations, because the three instructions subordinate to while were executed 13 times.

Program 9 - Compute the Value of the H Series = 1 + (1 / 2) + (1 / 3) + ... + (1 / N)

#P009: repetition with the while command (second example)

N = 5

H = 1

i = 1 #control variable

print('* * * calculation of H = 1 + (1 / 2) + (1 / 3) + ... + (1 / N), data N =',N)

44

while (i !=N): i = i + 1

H = H + (1 / i)

print('* * * answer: H = ', H)

Output [9]:

```
* * * calculation of H = 1 + (1 / 2) +
(1 / 3) + ... + (1 / N), given N = 5
* * * reply: H = 2.28333333333333333
```

The break command can be used to break a loop "on the go," passing the program execution flow to the line that is located immediately after the end of the command block subordinate to the loop. In turn, the continue command serves to break an iteration, but not the loop itself. More clearly: whenever the continue is executed, the program execution flow is automatically diverted to the line containing the while command.

Program 10 – Loop Break with Break and Iteration Break with Continue

#P010: while com break + while com continue

print(' ') print('1-Example of while with break:\n')

n=-1;

while (n < 21): n=n+1;

if n%2 != 0: break # break the loop if n is odd...

45

```python
print(n)

print('end of the while with \n')

print(' ')

print('2-Example of while with continue:\n') n=-
1;

while (n < 21): n=n+1;

if n%2 != 0: continue #breaking the iteration if n
is odd...

print(n)

print('end of the while with \n')
```

Output [10]:

```
----------------------------------------
1-      Example of while with break:

0
end of while with break

----------------------------------------
2-      Example of while com continues:

0
```

```
2
4
6
8
10
12
14
16
18
20
```

end of while com continue

Vectorization

- Major data science packages allow operations on datasets without the need to implement loops. This process is known as vectorization and will be presented in the future book.

- For the reason given, although the while command is widely used in the programming of conventional systems, it is far less employed in data science.

Repeat Instructions (2): for - range ()

Like while, the for command also serves to implement code block repetition. It exists in virtually all programming languages and because it is more practical than while programmers usually choose it in situations where they want to execute a set of commands for a fixed number of times. In the Python language, for has a very unique (and relevant!) feature: it can only iterate on sequences. In this lesson, we'll show you how to use for to iterate over sequences created with the range() function. From Chapter III, we'll see how it's possible to use it to iterate over more complex sequences such as 'NumPy' lists, dictionaries, tuples, files, and arrays.

Program 11 - Basic Recipe to Implement the Loops using the for-range() structure

Attention: as the program shows, the final limit defined in a range() will not be part of the generated sequence (we will comment more about it in the text after the program code).

```
#P011: repeat with for-range() print('\n* *
printing from 0 to 9') for i in range(10):

print(i)


print('n* * printing from 100 to 105')


for i in range(100, 106):

print(i)


print('\n* * 0 to 15, using 5 as increment')
```

for i in range(0, 16, 5): print(i)

print('n* * reverse order: 5, 4, 3, 2, 1')

for i in range(5, 0, -1):

print(i)

Output [11]:

```
* printing from 0 to 9 0
1
2
3
4
5
6
7
8
9

* printing from 100 to 105 100
101
102
103
104
105

* * using 5 as 0 increment
5
10
15
```

```
*          * reverse order 5
4
3
2
1
```

The for-range() structure executes a loop for a fixed number of times. Controls subordinate to the fork shall be indented. You must specify:

- A control variable (or counter) is the popular "for the variable," which in our program was called "i" in the four loops implemented.

- The upper and lower limits and the increment value: these values determine the number of repetitions that the loop will contain and are set using the range() function. The explanation of this function is given below.

Knowing the Range() Function

The range() function is used to generate a sequence of integers that is generally used to be traversed by a for command. Table 4 provides detailed information on its syntax and parameters.

- Syntax: range ([start], end, [increment])

- Parameters:

    o start: start sequence number (optional). If omitted, the value 0 is assumed.

- o end: sequence will be generated up to, but not including, the number specified in this parameter (only required parameter).

- o increment: the difference between each number in the sequence (optional). If omitted, the value 1 will be used.

- Comments:

  - o All parameters must be of integer type;

  - o All parameters can be positive or negative;

  - o Range In the range () function and Python language, value sets are indexed from the value 0 and not from the value 1. In other words: in Python, the

  - o The first element of a sequence, list, vector, etc. will always have the index 0. It is for this is why the command like range (n) produces a list whose first element is 0 and the last n-1,

- Examples:

  - o range (3)   # [0,1,2]

  - o range (1.4)   # [1,2,3]

  - o range (0.10.2)   # [0,2,4,6,8]

To conclude the lesson, below, I am presenting a summary with the "recipe" to implement the most common cases of use of the for-range() structure.

- for simple: iteration from 0 to n-1 with an increment of 1

```
for (counter) in range (n):
        command1

        ...
        commandn
```

- for basic: iteration from 1 to n, increment 1

```
    for (counter) in range (1, n + 1):
command1

...
commandn
```

- for increasing: going from n to m (where m □ n), with an increment of

```
for (counter) in range (m, n + 1, k):
command1

...
commandn
```

- for decreasing: goes from m to n (where m ≥ n), with decreasing k

```
for (counter) in range (n, m-1, -k):
command1

...
commandn
```

Python or R?

The R and Python languages are definitely the most popular in the area of data science. The choice between one and the other depends basically on the profile of the work team and the type of project to be conducted. Chart 6 makes a small comparison between these two languages, trying to highlight the most important characteristics of each language, as well as its main advantages, disadvantages, and ways of use. You will find many texts on the Internet comparing these languages. In general, there is a consensus that both are very important, and it is observed in practice that many companies have been combining the two in their projects.

R	Python
R is a language created by statisticians for statisticians. The manuals use the vocabulary of statisticians, and the structure of the language favors those who have the "mind" of statisticians. So it's not always easy for computer scientists to assimilate.	Python is a language of computer scientists for computer scientists. It is a multiparadigm language that incorporates all modern aspects of system development. So it's usually more attractive to computer scientists.

R is a specific purpose language: it serves for data analysis.	Python is a language of general-purpose, serving not only for data analysis but also for the development of any type of system, such as Web sites, games, corporate systems, etc..
Basic data structures for data analysis, such as data frames and arrays, are part of the core of the R language.	Data frames and arrays are neither part of the core nor the *standard* Python *library*. They need to be incorporated into the language by installing packages for data analysis such as 'NumPy' and 'pandas.' It is also important to note that many popular Python packages reproduce and/or extend features present in R, MATLAB, and other languages typically used for scientific computing.
It is more difficult to integrate the R *scripts* with the other systems of a	Some companies prefer to use Python for data science exactly because

company. Normally, it becomes necessary to use some third party product/component.	the integration with the other systems of the company can be done directly.
R is an interpreted and interactive language.	Python is also interpreted and interactive.
In general, R is still somewhat more used for conducting "classical statistics" and data visualization projects.	Python is commonly used in projects involving artificial intelligence/*machine learning*.
Installation and management of packages are simpler in R: everything is done in a trivial way through the central CRAN repository. This is an attractive factor for those who are not computer professionals.	Installing Python and its packages is a bit more difficult. Also, the fact that there are many Python distributions often confuses people. However, Python also has a central repository called PyPi.
RStudio is, by far, the most widely used IDE for the development of R programs.	There is no IDE that is clearly the most popular among Python developers. There are many options like Spyder, Rodeo, and

	IPython (commonly used in data science projects) and PyDev (more suitable for general application development).
R has a large community of users. This community is extremely active in forums such as Stack Overflow.	Python also has a huge community of users, very active in Stack Overflow and other Internet forums.

Chapter Two

Creating and Using Functions

A Python function is nothing more than a block of code that gets a name, which allows it to be called (i.e., executed) multiple times in the same program. The functions were created due to a practical need common to many systems and applications: repeat a sequence of specific instructions in different parts of the program.

To make the concept clear, consider as an example, a computer game that displays a certain animation every time the player passes the stage. As this situation can occur several times during the same match, the code snippet responsible for designing the animation will certainly be implemented as a function (which could be called "animacao_passa_fase()," for example).

This chapter has two objectives. The first is to teach you how to program your own functions. The second is to introduce the mathematical and statistical functions of the standard library, a set of ready-made and very important functions for data science that you "get as a gift" when installing any Python distribution!

Creating Functions

A function is a block of named code, which can receive one or more values as input, called parameters or arguments. It usually returns some computed results based on these parameters (although, in Python, not all functions need to return results or receive input parameters).

The reserved word def is used for setting functions. More specifically, to create a function, you must start by typing the word def, then indicate the name of the function, its parameters (if any), and, finally, the block of code corresponding to the body of the function.

Program 12 - Definition of a Function Called "track_etaria"

This function takes as input the age of a person (integer) and returns as output its age range (string). The return command should be used to return the function value.

```
#P012: creating and using a function

def range_etaria(age):

if (age < 18) :

return '<18'

elif (age >= 18 and age < 30) :

return '18-29'
```

```
elif (age >= 30 and age < 40) :

return '30-39'

else :

return '>=40'


# Calling the function with different values for the parameter "age"

a = age_range(15) b = age_range(50) c = age_range(35)


print(a); print(b); print(c)
```

Output [12]:

```
<18
>=40
30-39
```

As you may have noticed, the program starts with the "range_etaria()" function setting (lines 2-10). The first line of the function definition, which contains the word def, is called the function header, while the following lines form its body. The header should end with ":" and the body should be indented. Once the function has been set, it can be used anywhere in the program. And that's exactly what we did! In Program 12, the "range_etaria()" function is called three times, filling in variables "a", "b" and "c":

a = age_range(15)

b = age_range(50)

c = age_range(35)

In the program body, the functions need to be defined before they are called. For this reason, you cannot, for example, place the "age_range (35)" command before the code that defines this function. See that the Spyder IDE complains itself when you try to do this.

Modules

There are two ways of using a function. The first is to create it and run it in the same program as we just did. The second is to define it in a file separate from the main program and then import it using the import command. In the Python world, a file containing only functions is named module.

Program 13 - Module Import

If you save a file called "my_functions.py," containing the definition of the function "track_etaria()," you can import it and use it as a Python module using the form shown in the program below.

> #P013: Importing and using a function from a module

```
import my_functions


a = my_functions.age_range(15) b =
my_functions.age_range(50) c =
my_functions.age_range(35)


print(a); print(b); print(c)
```

Output [13]:

```
<18
>=40
30-39
```

Comments:

- As shown, the way to use a function of a module
  is a bit different: you must write the name of the
  module, then a period (".") And the name of the
  function (e.g., my_functions.file_file (18)).

- The file name must have the extension ".py"
  (e.g., "my_functions.py"). However, when
  importing the module, ".py" should not be
  specified.

- A module can contain one or more functions.

- The file must be saved in the same folder as the
  program (s) that will use it or in a folder that is

visible from any other folder (in the Windows environment, it is one specified in the PATH environment variable).

Packages

- Python allows you to group collections of modules that contain similar or related functionality in a structure called a package. Other programs can also import the packages through the import command.

- In this book, we will not cover package creation. However, in subsequent chapters, We will show you how to work with several ready-made packages made available by WinPython obtained through PyPI.

Optional Parameters and the None Value

The functions can be defined with optional parameters, as shown in the example below.

Program 14 - Function with the Optional Parameter

In this program, the "sum_numbers()" function has three parameters ("x", "y", and "z"), but the third one takes the value None as default. This allows you to call the function by passing two or three numbers as a parameter. In the first case, it will return x + y and in the second case x + y + z.

```
# P014: Function with the optional parameter

def sum_number (x, y, z = None):

    if (z == None):

        return x + y

    else:

        return x + y + z

print (sum_number (1, 2))

print (sum_number (1, 2, 3))

Exit [14]:

3
6th
```

But what is None? This is a special value, which has its own type ("NoneType"), and can be understood as "absence of anything." Returning to the optional parameters, it is important to note that these should always be placed as the parameters of the last one in the function declaration. In addition to None, you can assign any other default value for the optional parameters. See the following example.

Program 15 - Function with Parameter that has Default Value

Definition of the "f_calculate()" function, whose third parameter ("operator") has the value "+" as default. If you call the function without passing the third parameter, the value "+" is automatically adopted.

#P015: another function with parameter that has a default value

```python
def f_calculate(x,y,operation='+'):

if (operation=='+'):

return x+y

elif (operation=='-'):

return x-y

elif (operation=='*'):

return x*y

elif (operation=='/'):

return x/y

else:

return invalid operation!


print(f_calculate(1, 2))# returns 1+2 = 3

print(f_calculate(1, 2, '+')) #return 1+2 = 3

print(f_calculate(1, 2, '-')) #return 1-2 = -1
print(f_calculate(1, 2, '*')) #return 1*2 = 2
```

print(f_calculate(1, 2, '/')) #return 1/2 = 0.5
print(f_calculate*(1, 2, '.')* #return 'invalid
operation

Output [15]:

```
3
3
-1
2
0.5
Invalid operation!
```

Procedures

In the previous examples, all defined functions returned some value using the return command. However, you can also use the def command to create functions that only perform some type of action, but do not return any values to the user. These functions do not have the return command.

Program 16 - Definition of a Function that does not Return a Value

The following example illustrates a Python program that has the function declaration "print_head()." Consider that it is used to print the string passed in "name" as the header for a hypothetical company's reports. It does not return any value when called! Instead, simply perform an action: print the header.

P016: Function that returns no value

65

```python
def print_header (name):

    print ("\ n --------------------------------------")

    print ("* * Report -" + name)

    print ("-------------------------------------- \ n")

print_header ('Bestsellers')

print_head ('Out of Stock')
```

Exit [16]:

```
----------------------------------------
* * Report - Top Selling Products
----------------------------------------
----------------------------------------
* * Report - Out of Stock Products
----------------------------------------
```

In other programming languages, reusable modules that do not return value are called procedure or void. But in Python, everything is considered to function, regardless of whether it returns value or not, as you can make sure when doing the "print_header()" type check:

```python
print(type(print_header))
```

Output [16]:

```
<class 'function'>
```

It is also important to make it clear that you can create functions without parameters. For example, if all the headers of the company's reports had a fixed message, the function "print_head()" would not need to have any parameter, as shown in the code below:

```
def print_header ():
  print ("\ n -------------------------
-------------")
  print ("* * * * Report * * * *")
  print ("-----------------------------
--------- \ n")
```

Parameter Values

In Python, when a variable of a primitive type (integer, float, string or boolean) is passed as an argument to a function and has its content changed within the function's code block, the change in question is not reflected the main program (for who called the function). To facilitate the understanding of this concept, we will present an example program that will be commented in detail.

Program 17 - Function Receiving a Primitive Type Variable as an Argument

P017: Parameter Pass - Variable of a Primitive Type

def sum_um (number):

 number = number + 1

 print ("I added one inside the function: the number)

```
k = 100

print ('original value of k:,' k)

soma_um (k)

print ('Finished the function and k didn't actually
change:,' k)

Exit [17]:
```

the original value of k: 100

I added one into the function: 101

Finished the function and k did not actually change: 100

Explanation:

- Initially, we have the definition of a very simple function, called "soma_um(numero)," a function-style-procedure, that is, that does not return value. This function takes as input a number, adds one to this number, and after the sum, prints its value.

- Then start the main program, with the instructions k=100 and print('original value of k:,' k). No news so far! Let's just take this opportunity to introduce a new concept: "k" is called a global variable, because it is a variable declared in the body of the main program. A variable declared within a function is, in turn, called a local variable.

- Next comes the command: soma_um(k), where the variable "k" is passed as an argument to "soma_um(numero)." With this, the value of "number" becomes the same as that of "k," i.e., 100. Within the function, "number" is incremented by one unit (goes to 101... the content of "number" is printed to leave no doubt!).

- However, when the function "dies" (at the end of its execution), see that this change was not reflected to "k" (as the last print() of the main program shows). More clearly: although "number" has changed from 100 to 101 within the "soma_um(numero)" function, the value of "k" has remained equal to 100 outside this function.

But why did it happen like this? The answer is quite simple. This is because, in the Python language, all function parameters that are associated with primitive types are always treated as value parameters. And whenever a variable is passed as a value parameter to a function, a temporary copy of it is automatically generated.

During the execution of the function, only this temporary copy is used. Thus, when the parameter value is changed, this only affects the temporary storage (the effect is local to the function). The variable outside the procedure (global variable, our "k" from the example) will never be touched.

Predefined Functions

The pre-defined functions (built-in functions) are those that are part of the Python language itself and can be used without having to import any module. In the previous chapter, we worked with three of them: type(), print(), and input(). Below nine more predefined functions are presented. In the notation used, consider that x is a parameter of type integer or float and that s is a parameter of type string:

Numeric Functions

- abs (x): returns the absolute value of x;

- pow (x, y): returns x raised to y.

- round (x, d): returns x rounded to d decimal places (in this case, x must be a float).

String Functions

- len (s): returns the length (number of characters) of s;

- max (s): returns the largest character of s, considering the lexicographic order;

- min (s): Returns the smallest character of s, considering the lexicographic order.

Type Conversion Functions

- float (s): convert the string s to a float. The variable s must contain a valid number, integer or float; otherwise, the function returns an error;

- int (s): Converts the string s to an integer. The variable s must contain an integer valid; otherwise, the function returns an error;

- str (n): Converts the number n to a string. Its use is necessary when you want to concatenate a string with a number.

Program 18 - Exemplifies the Use of Predefined Functions

```
#P018: predefined functions

#Numeric functions n1=100 n2=3.141592653
n3=9.99


print(abs(1000), abs(-500), abs(2 * -2.5), abs(0))
#0

print(pow(n1,2))#10000

print(round(n2,2))#3.14

print(round(n2), round(n3))#10
```

```python
#Conversion functions

s1='5' s2='9.99"


print(int(s1))#converted '5' -> 5

print(float(s2)) #converted '9.99' -> 9.99

print('The value of 10 digit PI is: ' + str(n2)))
print('The value of 2 digit PI is: ' +
str(round(n2,2)))


#functions of string s1='python'
s2='unconstitutional".


print(len(s1))#6

print(len(s2))#16

print(max(s1))#'y'

print(min(s1))#'h'
```

Output [18]:

```
1000 500 5.0 0
10000
3.14
3 10
5
```

```
9.99
```

The value of PI with 10 digits is 3.141592653 The value of PI with 2 digits is: 3.14

```
6
16
y
h
```

Math Module

The 'math' module is one of many that are part of the standard library. Therefore, it is automatically installed by any Python distribution (CPython, Anaconda, WinPython, etc.). This module provides several useful mathematical functions and constants, such as rounding, trigonometric, logarithmic, etc. functions. Before using it, you need to import it using the command shown below:

import math

Below some of the main constants and functions provided by the 'math' module 9 are listed, respectively. The following is a program that exemplifies their use.

'Math' module constants:

- math.pi: mathematical constant 3.14159;

- math.e: mathematical constant 2.718281 (Euler number);

- math.tau: mathematical constant 6.283185 (equivalent to 2π);

- math.inf: float value representing $+\infty$. For $-\infty$ just use -math.inf;

- math.nan: This is the famous NaN, float value that represents "not a number." This value is generated by Python whenever a number cannot express the result of a calculation. Any calculation involving NaN will always result in NaN (eg 1 + NaN = NaN).

'Math' module functions:

Rounding Functions

- math.ceil (x): "up" rounding, i.e., returns the smallest integer with a value equal to or greater than x;

- math.floor (x): "down" rounding, i.e., returns the largest integer with a value equal to or less than x.

- math.trunc (x): truncation, which means limiting the number of digits of x.

Logarithmic / Exponential Functions

- math.exp (x): returns e raised to x;

- math.log2 (x): returns the logarithm of x in base 2;

- math.log10 (x): returns the logarithm of x in base 10;

- math.log (x, b): returns the logarithm of x in base b (according to the documentation of Python, should only be used when b is different from 2 and 10).

- math.pow (x, y): returns x raised to y;

- math.sqrt (x): returns the square root of x;

Trignometric Functions (in all of them, x is an angle that must be given in radians)

- math.acos (x): returns the cosine arc of x;

- math.asin (x): returns the sine arc of x;

- math.atan (x): returns the tangent arc of x;

- math.cos (x): returns the cosine of x;

- math.sin (x): returns the sine of x;

- math.tan (x): returns the tangent of x;

- math.degrees (x): converts the x angle from radians to degrees;

- math.radians (g): converts the angle g from degrees to radians.

Hyperbolic Functions

- There are also analogous hyperbolic functions, whose names always end with the letter "h." Ex .: math.tanh (x) returns the hyperbolic tangent of x.

Values Testing Functions

- math.isnan (x): Returns True if x is NaN; otherwise False is returned;

- math.isfinite (x): returns True if x is not infinite and neither NaN; otherwise, False is returned;

- math.isinf (x): re

Program 19 - Exemplifies the Use of Constants and Functions of the 'math' Module

```
#P019: 'math' module

import math

# Constant PI

print('PI=',math. pi)#3.141592653589793


#Rounding functions

x1 = 5.9

print('\n') print(x1)
```

```
print('ceil',math. ceil(x1)) print('floor',math.
floor(x1)) print('trunc',math. trunc(x1))


#logarithm print('n') x2 = 1024

print('log of ',x2, 'in base 2: ', math.log2(x2))


#prints table with sine, cosine and tangent of 30,
45 and 60 #note that it is necessary to convert
the angles to radian print('\n')

for angle_degrees in range(30,61,15):
angle_radians = math. radians(angle_degrees)
print('\n* * * Angulo=',angle_degrees, '
degrees')

print('SENO=',round(math.
sin(angle_radians),2))
print('COSSENO=',round(math.
cos(angle_radians),2))
print('TANGENTE=',round(math.
tan(angle_radians),2))
```

```
Output [19]:
PI= 3.141592653589793

5.9
ceil 6
floor 5
truncated 5
```

```
log of 1024 in base 2: 10.0

*        * * Angle= 30 degrees SENO= 0.5
COSSENO= 0.87
TANGENT= 0.58

*        * * Angle= 45 degrees SENO= 0.71
COSSENO= 0.71
TANGENT= 1.0

*        * * Angle= 60 degrees SENO= 0.87
COSSENO= 0.5
TANGENT= 1.73
```

Statistics Module

This module provides functions for basic statistical calculations10 on datasets. The data to be processed must be specified as lists of values. Functions for the calculation of central tendency and variability measures are offered, as presented below (consider that the parameter "lst" is a data set represented in a list).

Statistics module functions:

- statistics.mean (lst): average of lst values;

- statistics.median (lst): median of lst (a nice thing is that values are not need to be sorted);

- statistics.harmonic_mean (lst): harmonic mean;

- statistics.mode (lst): mode of a list of discrete values;

- statistics.median_low (lst): when lst has an even number of values, returns the smallest of the two values that would be used to compute the median. Example: for [1,2,3,4], returns 2;

- statistics.median_high (lst): when lst has an even number of values, returns the largest of the two values that would be used to compute the median. Example: for [1,2,3,4], returns 4;

- statistics.median_grouped (lst): returns the median of continuous data grouped, calculated as the 2nd quartile, using interpolation;

- statistics.stdev (lst): sample standard deviation;

- statistics.pstdev (lst): population standard deviation;

- statistics.variance (lst): sample variance;

- statistics.pstdev (lst): population variance;

Program 20 - Exemplifies the Use of the Functions of the Statistics Module

IMDb (https://www.imdb.com/) is a well-known cinema website that stores complete information about hundreds of thousands of movies. Among these films are those directed by Milos Forman, a filmmaker who won an Oscar for best director on two occasions? IMDb allows your users to assign notes for movies, which can range from 0 to 10. When a user searches for information about a movie, the IMDb also displays the average rating score of the users. In the case of director Milos Forman, for films directed by him after 1970, we have the following average ratings:

Movie	Public Note (average)
Insatiable Search (1971)	7.4
A Stranger in the Nest (1975)	8.7
Hair (1979)	7.6
In the Ragtime Season (1981)	7.3
Amadeus (1984)	8.3
Valmont - A History of Seductions (1989)	7.0
The People Against Larry Flint (1996)	7.3

The World of Andy   7.4
(1999)

Shadows of Goya (2006)   6.9

Double placená procházka 6.7
(2009)

The program listed below creates two lists of values, called "movie_names" and "movie_evaluation," which receive the names and evaluations of the movies. We then show how to use the statistics module to compute the mean, median, variance, and standard deviation of the evaluations. Note that a nickname was assigned to the 'statistics' module at the time of import (import statistics as s). This was so that it would be possible to use its functions by simply writing the letter 's' instead of 'statistics' (nicknaming is not mandatory, we did this just because 'statistics' is a very big word!).

#P020: 'statistics' module

import statistics as s

names_films = ['Insatiable Search (1971)', 'A Stranger in the Nest (1975)',

Hair (1979),

In Ragtime Time (1981), Amadeus (1984),

Valmont - A History of Seductions (1989)', 'The People Against Larry Flint (1996)',

'The World of Andy (1999)', 'Shadows of Goya (2006)',

Dobre placená procházka (2009)]]

evaluation_films = [7.4, 8.7, 7.6, 7.3, 8.3, 7.0, 7.3, 7.4, 6.9, 6.7]

```
print('mean = ',s. mean(evaluation_films)))
print('median = ',s. median(evaluation_films))
print('variance = ',s. variance(evaluation_films))
print('standard deviation = ',s. stdev(evaluation_films))
```

Output [20]:

```
average = 7.46
median = 7.35
variance = 0.3804444444444443 standard
deviation = 0.61680178699842
```

'Random' Module

This module offers a series of functions for random number generation. Some examples are given below:

Random Module Functions:

- random.random (): returns a real number (float) in the range [0.0, 1.0). This notation indicates that 0.0 can be generated, but 1.0 cannot;

- random.randint (start, end): returns an integer in the range [start, end);

- random.choice (sequence): draws an element from a sequence;

- random.seed (seed): used to define a seed in experiments reproducible. When the seed is not specified, it is assigned according to the system timestamp (date and time, nanosecond precision);

- random.getstate (): captures the current state of the random number generator (plus Program 21).

- random.setstate (e): used to return the generator to state and previously captured by the getstate () function.

Program 21 - Exemplifies the Use of the Functions of the 'Random' Module

Pay special attention to the recipe that should be used to work with seeds.

```
#P021: 'random' module

random import


#(1)-randint() function

for i in range(6):

n = random. randint(1,61) #Next mega-seine
numbers???

print(n)


#(2)-function choice()

k = random. choice([1,2,3,4,5])

print(k)


#(3)-working with seeds

#When the seed is not specified, Python uses the
system timestamp #, and the values of n1 and n2
will change whenever the program is run
n1=random. random()
```

n2=random. random() print(n1, n2)

#? But if you specify the seed, the series of numbers will always be the same:

state = random. getstate() random. seed(2019)

x1=random. random()#0.8323...

x2=random. random()#0.7889...

print(x1, x2) random. setstate(state)

#IMPORTANT: to be able to "disable" the seed (return to the default value, i.e.

#the system timestamp), it is necessary to use the recipe shown above:

#

1 -> capture the defaut state of the generator (which is the system timestamp),

Using getstate()

2 -> change the seed with seed()

3 -> return to default generator state using setstate

Output [21]:

```
23
42
59
10
33
6


1

0.340729993052193  0.12938782726427955
0.8323024001314224  0.7889290619064494
```

It is worth accessing the complete documentation13 of the 'random' module to know other interesting functions. In addition, it is important to know that there are two other mathematical modules in the standard library: 'fractions' (implementation of numerical operations for rational numbers) and 'decimal' (arithmetic of real numbers with fixed or floating-point representation). Not to mention the 'NumPy' library, the theme of the next book of this series, which is responsible for providing a rich set of tools for the efficient manipulation of vectors and matrices.

Print () function

The print() function is for printing one or more objects (messages, numbers, lists, etc.) on the default output device, which is usually the computer's video monitor. This function has been used in all code examples presented so far, but only in a basic way. The following is a program that shows other possibilities of use.

Program 22 - Parameters and Operators that can be Used to Enrich the Functionalities of the Print() Function

```
#P022: print() revisited

a=1; b=2; c=3


#Prints values of "a", "b" and "c" separated by space

print(a,b,c)#1 2 3


#sep" parameter: exchange space for specified separator

print(a,b,c,sep=';')#1;2;3


#The special operator %s allows the creation of a formatted output #It has two operands: the formatted string and a value v=3.14

print("PI=%s" % v)#PI=3.14

#The escape sign (\) also allows you to print quotes ("Printing quotes \")#printing quotes "
print('Printing quotes \")# Printing quotes.'
```

```python
# Adding line breaks with \n
print ("line1\line2\line3")


# Separating values by tabulation with \t
print("column1\tcolumn2\tcolumn3")
```

Output [22]:

```
1 2 3
1;2;3
PI=3.14
Printing quotes " Printing quotes '
line1
line2 lire3
column1 column2 column3
```

Help () function

The help() function displays a help text about a particular command, function, or method of the Python language.

help(len)#shows the help of the len() function

Help on built-in function len in module builtins:

len(obj, /)

Return the number of items in a container.

import statistics

help(statistics.median_low) #shows the help of the 'median_low' function of the module

#'statistics' (module needs to be imported)

Help on function median_low in module statistics:

median_low(date)

Return the low median of numeric data.

When the number of data points is odd, the middle value is returned. When it is even, the smaller of the two middle values is returned.

median_low([1, 3, 5])

3

median_low([1, 3, 5, 7])

3

Chapter Three

Native Data Structures

Data structures (DS) are used to organize and store related data sets to allow them to be processed efficiently by different algorithms. As a data scientist, you will often need to work with DS to be able to study or transform databases.

DS can be divided into two categories: primitive and non-primitive (also called complex or aggregate). We already know the primitive structures very well, they are simply the common variables that store atomic values (that is, simple and indivisible values) of the type int, float, string, or boolean. For example, a string variable that stores a person's name and a float variable that stores their salary.

Aggregate structures, on the other hand, are far more advanced. They can store collections of related values, organizing them, always in some "smart" way, in different cells. An example of such a structure would be a memory table containing the names and salaries of all employees in a company, with the data arranged in ascending order of salary. In modern programming languages such as Python, aggregate DSs usually come with several useful methods to facilitate their operation ("method" is just a more stylish name for function!).

In this chapter, you will learn how to work with the four native aggregate structures of the Python language: lists, tuples, sets, and dictionaries. Once you have completed the chapter, you will have a solid understanding of the main features of each of them, as well as their main types of operations and practical use cases. This knowledge is very important to master Python's data science-specific packages, such as 'NumPy' and 'pandas,' which offer even more sophisticated aggregate DSs.

Lists

A list is an ordered sequence of elements, each associated with a number responsible for indicating its position. This number is called an index. The first key figure in a list is always 0, the second 1, and so on. Python's lists are similar to the vectors of other programming languages, such as Java or C, but are a little more flexible. To create a list, simply specify a sequence of values in square brackets, where a comma must separate the values. Here are some examples:

```
writers = ['Arnest Hemingway', 'Tony Morrison',
'Mark Twain'] sequence_fibonacci = [0,1, 1, 2,
3, 5, 8, 13, 21, 34, 55]

empty_list = []
```

The elements of a list need not be of the same type. For example, the following list contains values of type string, float, and even a sublist:

mixed_state = ['Anna', 9: 5, [10, 20, 30]]

Operations on Lists

Program 23 - Operations of Indexing, Slicing, Iteration, Search and Modification in List

This program defines a list called "lst_bugs" whose elements are some animals that live in Rio de Janeiro and are not as scary as the Python snake! The program presents several different ways to access the elements and to generate sublists that represent "clippings" of the list. The first operation is known as indexing and the second as slicing. We also present the basic way to scroll through a list in sequence (iteration operation) and to search for and modify its elements.

```
# P023: Basic List Processing

lst_animals = ['I love you', 'otter', 'sanderling', 'iguana']

size_list = len (lst_animals) #our known len () function can be used to

 #obtain list size (number of elements)

# (1) -indexing the elements
```

```
first = lst_animals [0] #returns 'I saw you'

last = lst_animals [3] # returns 'iguana'

last_too = lst_animals [-1] # also returns 'iguana'

print ('lst_animals:', lst_animals)

print ('data type:', type (lst_animals))

print ("total elements:", size_list)

print ("first element:" + first)

print ("last element:" + last)

print ("last element again:" + last_too)

print ('---------------')
```

56

```
# (2) -iteration: traversing elements with a for-range () loop

k = 1;

for b in lst_animals:

 print ('element', k, '=', b)

 k = k + 1

print ('--------------')

# (3) -factoring: getting slices
```

```python
print (lst_animals [0: 2]) # ['I love you', 'otter']

print (lst_animals [2: 4]) # ['sanderling', 'iguana']

print (lst_animals [: 2]) # ['I love you', 'otter']

print (lst_animals [2:]) # ['sanderling', 'iguana']

print ('---------------')

# (4) -operator in (search): element belongs to
list?

tem_otter = 'otter' in lst_animals

tem_python = 'python' in lst_animals

print ("'otter' is listed? ->", tem_otter)

print ("'python' is listed? ->", tem_python)

# (5) -modifying content

lst_animals [2] = 'savory' #changes index
element 2

print ("new list ->", lst_animals)

lst_animals [: 2] = ['weevil', 'guineapig']
#changes elements 0 and 1

print ("brand new list ->", lst_animals)

Exit [24]:
```

lst_animals: ['I love you', 'otter', 'sanderling', 'iguana']

data type: <class 'list'>

total elements: 4

first element: I saw you

last element: iguana

last element again: iguana

----

element 1 = I saw you

element 2 = otter

element 3 = sanderling

element 4 = iguana

['I have seen you', 'otter']

['sanderling', 'iguana']

['I have seen you', 'otter']

['sanderling', 'iguana']

Is 'otter' on the list? -> True

Is 'python' on the list? -> False

new list -> ['I love you', 'otter', 'loons', 'iguana']

Brand New List -> ['weevil', 'guineapig', 'loons', 'iguana']

The following is a brief explanation of the program, which is divided into five parts:

- The first one shows that brackets "[ ]" are used to access elements of a list. Within them, you specify an integer that corresponds to the key figure of the element that you wish to access. If you specify a negative number, Python indexes it backward, i.e., -1 takes the last element in the list, -2 the penultimate, etc.

- In the second part, we show you how to use the for...in structure to scroll through a list. The code block subordinate to the loop will be executed once for each element of the list. Note that with each iteration, variable "b" (iteration variable) automatically receives one of the elements in the list.

- The third part is the most interesting, thus deserving detailed comments. It demonstrates the notation used by Python for the slicing operation. In this type of operation, you can get a sublist from any list using the syntax shown below.

List Slicing Operation Syntax - Most Common Practical Situations

- o Slicing operation of an "lst" list:

- o lst [i: j]: from index element i to index j-1.

- o lst [i:]: from index element i to the last one in the list.

- o lst [: j]: from the first list element (index 0) to index element j-1.

- o lst [i: j: k]: from index element, i to maximum index j-1 using step k.

- o lst [-k:]: Get the last k elements of the list.

- o lst [: - k]: In a list of n elements, returns the first n-k elements.

- In Part 4, we show that the in operator can be used to test whether a particular element belongs to the list (True or False will be returned).

- Finally, Part 5 presents the basic procedure for changing the contents of the list. See what we can modify a single element, just indicate its index, or several at once, using the same notation used in the slicing operation.

Program 24 - Two Other Operations Allowed on Lists: Repetition and Concatenation

#P024: repeating and concatenating lists

lst1 = ['Denver','CO']

lst2 = ['USA']

#repetition: operator *

print(lst1*3)
#['Denver','CO','Denver','CO','Denver','CO']

#concatenation: operator +

print(lst1 + lst2) #['Denver','CO','USA']

['Denver', 'CO', 'Denver', 'CO', 'Denver', 'CO']

['Denver', 'CO', 'USA']

Methods

Besides being an ED, a Python list is also an object. As the name indicates, the object is a concept related to the paradigm of object-oriented programming, briefly discussed in the first chapter.

Fortunately, for our joy, we don't need to understand anything about object-oriented programming to use the objects of the Python language. Just know that every object is an ED that contains data (in the case of a list, its elements) and methods (functions present "inside" the object and that are always available for use by the programmer).

As with normal functions (such as len(), type(), etc.), a method can receive zero or more arguments and will return a value. The difference is that, to call a method, we must add a period (".".") and the name of the method at the end of the list in object-oriented programming terminology, this is called "invoking" the method (a somewhat ugly name, but not as terrible as "indentation"). Some of the most important methods available for lists are shown below. In the adopted rating, consider that "lst" is a list and "and" an element.

Methods Available for Lists

- lst.append(e): adds the "e" element to the "lst";

- lst.clear(): removes all elements from the list;

- lst.count(e): counts the number of occurrences of "e" in "lst";

- lst.extend(lst2): insert the "lst2" list at the end of "lst";

- lst.index(e): returns the lowest index of "e" in "lst";

- lst.insert(pos, e): insert the object "e" in the "pos" position of "lst";

- lst.remove(e): remove the "e" element from "lst";

- lst.reverse(): inverts the list;

- lst.sort(): sort the "lst" elements.

Program 25 - Exemplifies the Use of ED Methods List

```
#P025: methods available for number lists = [0,
10, 15, 10, 20] print("original list: ", numbers)


how many_10 = numbers.count(10) #returns 2

print("num. of occurrences of value 10: ",
quantos_10)


i_10 = numbers.index(10) #returns 1

print("index of the first occurrence of 10: ",
i_10)


numbers.append(5)#adds the value 5 to the end
of the list

print("modified list1: ", numbers)
```

numbers.insert(1,1000) #insert 1000 as second element

print("modified list4: ", numbers)

numbers.remove(10) #remove the first element 10

print("modified list3: ", numbers)

numbers.extend([50, 60]) #adds list [50, 60] at the end

print("modified list5: ", numbers)

numbers.sort() #order

print("ordered list: ", numbers)

numbers.reverse() #inverte

print("reverse list: ", numbers)

numbers.clear() #empty the list

print("empty list: ", numbers)

Output [25]:

original list: 0, 10, 15, 10, 20] num. of occurrences of value 10: 2 index of the first occurrence of 10: 1

     modified list1: [0, 10, 15, 10, 20, 5]

     modified list4: [0, 1000, 10, 15, 10, 20, 5]

     changed list3: [0, 1000, 15, 10, 20, 5]

     modified list5: [0, 1000, 15, 10, 20, 5, 50, 60]

     ordered list: [0, 5, 10, 15, 20, 50, 60, 1000]

     reverse list: [1000, 60, 50, 20, 15, 10, 5, 0]

     empty list: []

Predefined Functions and Lists

Some predefined Python functions can be directly applied over lists, allowing you to perform certain operations without the need to create loops. These are presented below.

Predefined Functions that Can be Used in Lists

- sum(lst): sum the elements of the list (only for lists with numeric elements);

- min(lst), max(lst): return, respectively, the lowest and highest value of "lst" (for any kind of list);

- len(lst): returns the size of the list.

Program 26 - Using Predefined Functions in Lists

Below are the IQ test results of eight participants in a study.

Interviewee	IQ
Asif	126
Bill	100
Bob	130
Jim	92
Liu	120
Joan	99
Rakesh	125
Zangh	72

The following program shows how to use predefined functions to compute the maximum, minimum and average IQ.

#P026: applying predefined functions on lists

lst_qi = [126, 100, 130, 92, 120, 99, 125, 72]

print("IQ test results: ", lst_qi)

print("bigger: ", max(lst_qi))

print("smaller: ", min(lst_qi))

```
print("sum: ", sum(lst_qi))
```

```
print("media: ", sum(lst_qi) / len(lst_qi))
```

Output [26]:
```
IQ test results: [125, 92, 72, 126, 120,
99, 130, 100]
largest: 130
smaller: 72
sum: 864
average: 108.0
```

Lists and the Statistics Module

- Do not forget that all functions of the statistics module (shown in 'Statistics Module' lesson) can also be directly applied to lists. Among them, functions for the calculation of variance, standard deviation, median, mode, etc.

List Comparison

Comparison operators can be used in lists, tuples (see next section), strings, and other types of sequences. The comparison begins with the first element of each sequence. If they are equal, the second element will be compared and so on, until different elements are found. Subsequent elements are ignored. Examples:

1,2,3] > [1, 5, 10]#returns False

20] > [10, 998, 800]#return True

Cloning a List

Suppose you have an "a" list and want to generate a copy of it in another "b" list. In this situation, you should not use the command below at all:

- b = a

What do you mean? What happens is that, in Python, every assignment operation involving complex objects (basically, anything other than a primitive ED) will not result in the creation of a new object. Instead, the assignment will only create a new variable that refers to the original object. In computer jargon, this process is called a shallow copy.

However, in many practical situations, you may be interested in the operation known as a deep copy, which consists of creating a real copy or a clone of an object. In this case, Python offers two outputs:

- Slicing: the slicing operation of lists always generates clones (i.e., the sublists generated are always real copies of the data of a list). This way, using the command b = a[:], you can get a sublist that is actually a complete copy of the original list.

- Module 'copy': offers a function called deepcopy() to make a deep copy not only of lists but of any complex object: b = copy.deepcopy(a).

Program 27 - Making the Clean Copy and Cloning of Lists

```python
#P027: shallow copy (reference) x deep copy
(cloning)

import copy


#1-Shallow Copy

print('* * * SHALLOW COPY') a = [1,2,3,4,5]

b = a

print('-a=',a)

print('-b=',b)


b[0] = 999

print('t-a',a)

print('\t-b:',b)

print('\t-a is b?',a is b)#True (the operator "is"
checks if two objects

#have the same reference)

print('\n ')
```

#2-Deep Copy using the slicing technique

print('* * * DEEP COPY WITH FACT') c = [1,2,3,4,5]

d = c[:]

print('-c=',c)

print('-d=',d) d[0] = 999

print('t-c:',c)

print('\t-d:',d)

print('t-c is d?',c is d)#False

print('\n ')

#3-Deep Copy using 'copy' print('* * DEEP COPY WITH MODULE \'copy\'") and = copy.deepcopy(c)

print('-c=',c)

print('-e=',e) e[0] = 999

print('t-c:',c)

print('t and:',e)

print('t-a is b?',c is d)#False

107

Output [27]:

```
* * SHALLOW COPY
-a= [1, 2, 3, 4, 5]
-b= [1, 2, 3, 4, 5]
-a [999, 2, 3, 4, 5]
-b: [999, 2, 3, 4, 5]
-a is b? True


-------------------------------------
* DEEP CCPY WITH SLICING
-c= [1, 2, 3, 4, 5]
-d= [1, 2, 3, 4, 5]
-c: [1, 2, 3, 4, 5]
-d: [999, 2, 3, 4, 5]
-c is d? False


-------------------------------------
* * DEEP COPY WITH THE 'copy' MODULE
-c= [1, 2, 3, 4, 5]
-e= [1, 2, 3, 4, 5]
-c: [1, 2, 3, 4, 5]
-e: [999, 2, 3, 4, 5]
-a is b? False
```

Lists as Function Arguments

In 'Creating Roles' Lesson, we saw that when a variable that stores a primitive value (int, float, string, or boolean) is passed as an argument to a function, it is always a value parameter. This means that any changes in the contents of the variable that have been made inside the function's code block will not be reflected in the main program.

Conversely, if a complex object (such as a list, dictionary, set, etc.) is passed as an argument to a function, it will always be a reference parameter. This means that changes made to the format or content of the object will be permanent, i.e., they will be reflected in the main program. This behavior is automatic and cannot be modified (unlike what happens in "root" languages such as C and Pascal).

Program 28 - Passing a Complex Object Type (list) as Function Argument

```
#P028: function arguments:

#Variable of primitive type (int) x object of complex type (list)

def f_dummy(z):

if type(z) == list: z[0] = 999

else:

z = 999

x = 0

lst = [1,2,3,4,5]

print('x before calling the function f_dummy:',x)
f_dummy(x)

print('x after calling the function f_dummy:',x)
```

```
print(' ')
```

```
print('lst before calling the function
f_dummy:',lst) f_dummy(lst)
```

```
print('lst after calling function f_dummy:',lst)
```

Output [29]:

```
x before calling function f_dummy: 0 x
after calling function f_dummy: 0
-----------------------------------------
lst before calling function f_dummy: [1,
2, 3, 4, 5]
lst after calling function f_dummy:
[999, 2, 3, 4, 5]
```

Reference Parameters versus Value Parameters

- The changes in the reference parameters are permanent because internally, Python passes to the function, not a copy of the object, but the address of the object in memory. That is: the argument of the function and the object passed as parameter share the same address of memory. Therefore, a change in the former is permanently reflected in the latter.

- The value parameters work entirely differently: a temporary copy of the variable passed as a parameter is stored in some free memory location. During the execution of the function, only this temporary copy is used. If the value of the parameter is changed, that only affects temporary storage. The variable outside the procedure will never be touched.

Tuples

Like the lists, tuples represent a sequence of values indexed by integers. However, there is a crucial difference between these two data structures: tuples are immutable, i.e., they cannot have their elements changed. Therefore, they can be used as dictionary keys (see the lesson immediately after the next one), among other types of roles that cannot be played by lists.

Program 29 - Basic Creation and Manipulation of a Tuple-Type ED

See which parentheses should be used to create the tuple.

#P029: tuples - basic creation and manipulation

#tuple with 5 elements

t1 = (10, 20, 30, 40, 50)

To create a tuple with a single element,

A comma is used at the end

t2 = (100,)

#tupla empty - tuple() is the tuple constructor method.

t3 = tuple()

#if a sequence is passed to tuple(e.g. string or list),

#? the tuple is created with the elements of the sequence

t4 = tuple('DATA')#('D','A','D','O','S')

print('t1: ', t1)

print('data type: ', type(t1)) print('t1[0] -> ', t1[0])#10

print('t1[2:] -> ', t1[2:])#(30,40,50)

print('t2: ', t2)

print('t3: ', t3)

print('t4: ', t4)

Output [29]:
```
t1: (10, 20, 30, 40, 50)
data type: <class 'tuple'> t1[0] -> 10
t1[2:] -> (30, 40, 50)
```
112

```
t2: (100,)
t3: ()
t4: ('D', 'A', 'D', 'O', 'S')
```

The operators * (repetition), + (concatenation), in (pertinence test) also work for tuples, as do the functions len(), min(), max() and sum(). However, if you try to change a tuple, you will get an error because the tuple is unchangeable:

```
t1[0] = 1000
```

TypeError: 'tuple' object does not support item assignment

An interesting feature of the Python language is known as tuple assignment. It corresponds to the ability to assign values to more than one variable in a single line, using the syntax shown below:

```
a, b = ('Bob', 'Marley')
print(a)
print(b)
Out[1]:
Bob
Marley
```

Tuples vs. Lists

- The difference between tuples and lists is that tuples are immutable, while lists are not. This means that once defined and a tuple cannot have values entered, removed, or modified. At first, the "immutability" of tuples may seem meaningless. Still, it's actually a very useful feature in situations where you need to share data with an external function or program, but don't want your data to be modified.

- In addition, experiments reported in articles involving real and artificial databases have shown that for most search operations, tuples are more efficient (faster) than lists.

Sets

A set is an unordered collection of elements. Unlike lists and tuples, sets cannot have duplicate elements (i.e., a given element will appear 0 or 1 time in a set). Since the concept of sorting into assemblies does not exist, its elements do not have a key figure. To create a set, just specify a sequence of values between keys, separating them by a comma. See some examples:

```
genres = {'Drama', 'Romance', 'Action',
'Adventure'} numbers = {1, 2, 3, 4, 5, 6, 7, 8, 9,
10}

set_empty = set()
```

If we try to create a set with repeated elements, Python will remove the repetitions automatically:

```
x = {1, 1, 1, 1, 2}#results in {1, 2}
```

The set() function can also be used to make it possible to create sets from sequences (lists, tuples or strings):

```
y = set("DATA")#results in {'D', 'A', 'O', 'S'}
```

Python sets have the same meaning as mathematical sets. Thus, the main operations on this type of ED are the traditional ones of mathematics - union, intersection, difference, pertinence ratio, and inclusion ratio (the popular "contains/is contained"). Also, there are the methods to include and remove elements; finally, we can also iterate on the elements of a set using the for command.

Program 30 - Creation and Basic Manipulation of a Joint Type ED

P030: Sets - Basic Creation and Manipulation

#define 3 sets

a = {0,1,2,3}

b = {2,3,4,5}

c = {1,2}

intersection (&), union (|), difference (-) and symmetric difference (^)

print (a & b) # {2,3}

print (a | b) # {0,1,2,3,4,5}

print (a - b) # {0}

```
print (a ^ b) # {0,1,4,5}


# is contained (<=), contains (> =)

print ('')

print (c <= a) #True

print (c <= b) #False

print (a> = d) #True


#pertence ´in), does not belong (not in)

print ('')

print (0 in a) #True

print (0 in b) #False

print (0 not in b) #True


#including (adding) and removing (remove)
elements;

print ('')

c.add (10)

c.add (20)
```

print (c) # {1,2,10,20} c.remove (10)

print (c) # {1,220}

emptying a set (clear) and making deep copy (copy)

print (")

c.clear ()

print (c) #set ()

d = a.copy ()

print (d) # (0,1,2,3)

#iteration

print (")

for item in b:

print (item)

Oct [30]:

{2,3}

{0, 1, 2, 3, 4, 5}

{0, 1}

{0, 1, 4, 5}

True False True

True False True

{1, 2, 10, 20}

{1, 2, 20}

----

set ()

{0, 1, 2, 3}

2

3

4

Dictionaries

A dictionary is an ED in which the elements are key:value pairs. The key identifies an item, and the value stores its contents. Any stored value can be retrieved extremely quickly through its key.

One of the fundamental differences between dictionaries and lists is that, in a list, the indexes that determine the position of the elements must be integers, while in a dictionary, the indexes can be not only integers but also of any basic unchangeable type, such as strings and tuples. Another difference is that in a conventional dictionary, there is no concept of order; that is, it is an unordered collection of key:value pairs. Here are some examples of dictionary statements:

dic_students =
{'M01':'Jane','M13':'George','M15':'Thomas','M0
4':'Aldous'} dic_titulos =
{'Portela':22,'Mangueira':19,'Beija-Flor':14}
dictionary_ empty = {}

Notice that: (i) "{ }" keys were used to create the dictionary; (ii) within the keys, the colon symbol ":" is used to separate the key from its value; and (iii) the different elements are separated by commas.

Basic Operations

Program 31 - Operations of Insertion/Removal of Items, Search and Modification

The example illustrates the basic creation and manipulation of a student dictionary. In this dictionary, the key is the license plate, and the value is the student name. Basic dictionary operations are displayed: add and remove items, retrieve values, modify values, and search for a key that belongs to the dictionary.

```
#P031: Dictionary: basic creation and
manipulation dic_students =
{'M01':'Hane','M13':'George','M15':'Thomas'}
print('dic_students (original): ', dic_students)


#Insert new student (new key pair:value)

dic_students['M04'] = 'Aldous'


#Changes the value associated with key 'M01' to
Jane

dic_students['M01'] = 'Jane'


# Remove the key element 'M15'

of dic_students['M15']


# Checking if a key exists

tem_M13 = 'M13' in dic_students#returns True
tem_M99 = 'M99' in dic_students#returns False
```

print('dic_students (after changes): ',
dic_students)

print('data type: ', type(dic_students)) print('the
mat. M13?: ', has_M13) print('the mat. M99?: ',
has_M99)

In [31]:

dic_students (original): {'M01': 'Hane', 'M13':
'George', 'M15': 'Thomas'}

dic_students (after changes): {'M01': 'Jane',
'M13': 'George', 'M04': 'Aldous'} data type:
<class 'dict'>

exists mat. M13?: True exists mat. M99?: False.

Methods and Techniques of Iteration

Below I present some of the main methods available for
dictionaries. In the notation below, consider that "dic" is
a dictionary and "k" a key.

Methods Available for Dictionaries

- dic.keys(): returns a reference to all "dic" keys;

- dic.values(): returns a reference for all "dic"
  values;

- dic.items(): returns an object containing all {key:value} pairs of "dic";

- dic.clear(): removes all elements;

- dic.get(k): retrieves the value of the key element "k". If "k" does not exist, it returns None;

- dic.update(d): links the contents of a dictionary "d" to the dictionary "dic". If

- some "key:value" pair of "d" already exists in "dic", the information will be overwritten.

Program 32 - Use of Methods and Iteration on Dictionaries

IBGE's countries website (https:// países.ibge.gov.br/) allows comparing countries through their main demographic, social, economic and environmental indicators. Among the different information available is the total population of each country. The list below presents some examples:

Belize	179,014
Brazil	204,450,649
France	64,395,345
Mexico	127.017.224
New Zealand	2,213,123

| Portugal | 10,349,803 |
| Uruguay | 3,431,555 |

The following is a program that creates a dictionary where the key is the name of a country and the value of its population. The program makes use of the methods described in Table 15, as well as demonstrating how to proceed to iterate over a dictionary, i.e., to obtain all its keys and values. This operation is done using the items() method and the tuple assignment feature, presented at the end of Tuples section.

```
#P032: use of methods, functions, and iteration
over a dictionary


#(0)-Create the dictionary (for now without
Belize and New Zealand!)

d = {

Brazil: 204450649,

France: 64395345,

'Portugal':10349803, 'Mexico': 127017224,

Uruguay: 3431555,

}


#(1)-Using print('* * * 1-Methods * * *')
print(d) methods
```

```python
print(d.keys()) print(d.values())

print('The estimated population of Brazil is: ',
d.get("Brazil"))



#(2)-percurses all the elements of "d"

# At each iteration, the key is stored in "k" and
the value in "v"

print('') print('* * * 2-Progressing the dictionary
* * *') for k, v in d.items():

print(k, '->', v)



#(3)-Using the built-in functions:

#len(): counts the number of keys stored in the
dictionary

#min(): lower key value

#max(): higher key value

print(' ')

print('* * * 3-Using built-in functions * * *')
print('Total keys: ', len(d)) print('smallest key: ',
min(d))

print('largest key: ', max(d))
```

```
#(4)-Combining two dictionaries:

print(' ')

print('* * * 4-Combining Dictionaries * * * *')

d2 = {

Belize: 179014,

New Zealand: 2213123,

}


d.update(d2)

print('dictionary updated: ', d)


#(5)-removing all dictionary items

print('') print('* * * 5-Destroying a dictionary * *
*') d.clear()

print(d)
```

Output [32]:

```
* * * 1-Methods * * *
Brazil': 204450649, 'France': 64395345,
'Uruguay': 3431555, 'Mexico': 127017224,
'Portugal':
10349803}
```

```
dict_keys(['Brazil', 'France',
'Uruguay', 'Mexico', 'Portugal']))

dict_values([204450649, 64395345,
3431555, 127017224, 10349803]))
The estimated population of Brazil is:
204450649
-------------------------------------------
* * * 2-Running the dictionary * *
Brazil -> 204450649
France -> 64395345
Uruguay -> 3431555
Mexico -> 127017224
Portugal -> 10349803
-------------------------------------------
* * * 3-Using built-in functions * * *
Total keys: 5
smallest key: Brazil largest key:
Uruguay
-------------------------------------------
* * * 4-Combining Dictionaries * *
updated dictionary: {'Brazil':
204450649, 'France': 64395345,
'Uruguay': 3431555, 'Mexico':
127017224, 'Portugal': 10349803,
'Belize': 179014, 'New Zealand':
2213123}
-------------------------------------------
* * * 5-Destroying a dictionary * * *
{}
```

Chapter Four

Strings and Databases in Text Format

Most of the planet's digital information is available in text format: blogs, web pages, digital books, social networks, wikis, e-mails, CSV files, JSON files, etc. Thus, it is no surprise to note that, in recent years, the collection, processing, summarization, and analysis of digital text have become some of the most important tasks of data science.

With this scenario as motivation, this chapter is dedicated to the presentation of the basic techniques for word processing offered by the Python language. The content is divided into three parts:

- Part 1 - String treatment. It introduces the different methods and functions for processing string-like variables.

- Part 2 - Processing of databases in text format. Presents the techniques that can be employed to work with textual databases structured in different formats and coding standards.

- Part 3 - Regular expressions. It makes a brief introduction to regular expressions, a technique that allows a pattern to be specified (such a regular expression) and then used to scan a text to extract all the passages that "match" the pattern. This technique is very important in web scraping and text mining processes.

Strings

Although the string is one of Python's primitive types, it can also be manipulated as a tuple. This is exactly one of the features that make Python very advantageous for working with textual databases. More specifically, a Python string is considered a string of characters. For example, in the string 'Statistics,' the character 'E' occupies the index 0, 's' occupies the index 1, and so on. It is possible to access each character separately, using the operator brackets: "[ ]."

[0]	[1]	[2]	[3]	[4]	[5]	[6]	[7]	[8]	[9]	[10]
S	t	a	t	i	s	t	i	c	s	

Program 33 - Basic Techniques to Deal with Strings

See that it's just like the way we work with the lists and tuples.

```
#P033: basic string processing

word = 'Thou Blood.'
```

128

```
#(1) indexing characters

prim_letter = word[0]#return 'T' ult_letter =
word[len(word)-1]#return 'e' tot_letters =
len(word)#return 10
print(prim_letter,ult_letter,tot_letters)

print(' ')


#(2) obtaining segments or slices

print(word[0:3])#'Tie"

print(word[4:11])#'Blood"

print(word[:3])#'Tie"

print(word[4:])#'Blood"

print(word[-1])#'e' (last letter)

print(word[-2])#'u' (penultimate letter)

print(' ')


#(3) scrolling the string letter by letter, through a
loop

tot_esp = 0

for letter in word:
```

```
print(letter)

if letter == ' ':

tot_esp = tot_esp + 1

print("'" + word + "' has ' + str(tot_esp) + '
space(s)')

print(' ')
```

#(4) "in" operator

```
tem_a = 'a' in word #'Tie Blood' has the letter
'a'? tem_b = 'b' in word #'Tie Blood' has the
letter 'b'? print(tem_a, tem_b);
```

Output [33]:

T and 10

Tie Blood Tie Blood and

u

T i e

Blood

"Tie Blood" has 1 space(s)

True False

As with tuples, strings are "immutable," which means that it is not possible to change an existing string. The most you can do is create a new string that is a variation of the original. See the example below:

Wrong:	Right:
bug = 'Otter' bug [0] = 'K'	Animal = Otter new_big = 'K' + bug [1:] print (new_big)
TypeError: 'str' object does not support item assignment	**[1]** Otter

Methods

The next table lists some of the most important methods available for strings15. In the notation, consider that "s" is any string variable.

Methods Available for Strings

- s. lower(): returns a copy of converted "s" to lower case; important: this method, like all others, does not change the original string "s" since every string is immutable!

- s. upper(): returns a copy of "s" converted to uppercase;

- s. find(sub. start, end): checks if "sub" occurs in the string "s" or within a specific excerpt (if "start" and "end" have been defined). If so, it returns the index of the first occurrence. Otherwise, it returns -1;

- s. rfind(sub, start, end): equal to the find() method, but checks backward;

- s. endswith(suffix, start, end): checks whether "s" or a defined portion of "s" (if the optional parameters "start" and "end" have been specified) ends with the substring specified under "suffix." Return True or False;

- s. replace(sub_ant, sub_nova, max): returns a copy of the "s" string with the occurrences of the "sub_ant" substring replaced by "sub_nova." The parameter "max" can be used to determine the maximum number of changes to be made.

- s. count(sub, start, end): counts how many times the "sub" substring appears in the "s" section marked "start" and "end" (if these parameters are omitted, search the entire string).

- s. strip(): returns a copy of "s" without the blank spaces on the left and right;

- s. lstrip(): returns a copy of "s" without the blanks on the left;

- s. rstrip(): returns a copy of "s" without the left and right blank spaces;

- s. split(d, max): divides a string into a list of strings, according to the delimiter "d" (if not provided, use blank space). The parameter "max" can be used to determine the maximum number of elements in the list.

- s. translate(table, deletechars): this method is used to translate strings according to a translation table ("table" parameter) defined by the maketrans() method (the two methods work together). Its use is a bit complicated, and in this book, we will use it only in its basic form, where the "deletechars" parameter is used to remove characters from a string.

Program 34 - Methods Available for Strings

A note about the program below: there is no method to return the length of a string! To get this value, you need to use the old, good, predefined function len ().

```
#

P034: string methods

p1 = 'Iguana lizard.'


p1_maius = p1.upper() p1_minusc = p1.lower()


num_letters_p1 = len(p1) num_letters_a =
p1.count('a')

front_endswith = p1.endswith('rto', 4, 7)
front_find = p1.find('a')

front_rfind = p1.rfind('a')

p1_exchange = p1.replace('a', 'o') p1_split =
p1.split()


p2 = 'Otter';

test_strip = p2.strip();


p3 = 'hey, look at that... a otter!'

sem_punctuation = p3.translate(p3.maketrans('',
'', ',', .!')) #remove: , . !
```

```
      print("p1.upper()= " + p1_maiusc)
    print("p1.lower()= " + p1_minusc)
    print("len(p1)= " + str(num_letters_p1))
    print("p1.count('a')= " + str(num_letters_a))
    print("p1.endswith('rto',4,7)= ", front_endswith)
    print("p1.find('a')= ", front_find)
    print("p1.rfind('a')= ", front_rfind)
    print("p1.replace('a','o')= " + p1_troca)
    print("p1.split()= ", p1_split) print("p2.strip()=
    *" + teste_strip + "*") print("frase com
    punctuation= " + p3) print("phrase without
    punctuation= " + without_point)
```

Output[34]:

```
    p1.upper() = LIZARD IGUANA p1.lower() =
    lizard Iguana len(p1) = 12 p1.count('a')
    = 2 p1.endswith('rto', 4, 7) = True
    p1.find('a') = 1 p1.rfind('a') = 3
    p1.replace('a', 'o') = LIZARD Iguana
    p1.split() = ['LIZARD', 'Sanderling']
    p2.strip() = * Capivara *

    Phrase with punctuation = hey, look at
    that otter!
    Phrase without punctuation = hey look at
    that otter.
```

String Comparison

Comparison operators (==, !=, <, <=, >, >=) can be used with strings. However, the following rules must be observed:

- Two strings are equal only if they store the same word, written identically, including for upper and lower case letters.

- Programming languages do not "act" in the same way as people when making comparisons between strings! For programming languages, upper case letters come before lower case letters. This is because comparisons between strings are based on internal character codes, and upper case letters have lower case codes. For this reason, we often need to use the lower() (or upper()) method before comparing two strings.

- Similarly, accented characters have larger codes than lower case letters and numbers smaller codes than any letter. If you would like more information on this subject, search for "complete ascii table" and "unicode utf-8 table" on the Internet.

Program 35 - Strings Comparison

\#

P035: String comparison

p1 = 'bird'

p2 = 'SANDERLING'

p3 = '123'.

print(p1 == 'bird')# True

print(p1 === 'Pause')# False

print(p1 == p2)# False print(p1.lower() ==
p2.lower())# True print(p3 < p1)# True

p1 = 'aaa'

p2 = 'aaa'

p3 = 'AAA'.

print(p1 == p2)# False

print(p2 < p1)# True

print(p2 < p3)# False

Output[35]: True

```
False False True False True False True
False
```

String module

The string module is an old module of the standard library that offers a series of constants useful for handling strings.

Program 36 - Some Constants of the String Module

P036: string module

import string

print(string.ascii_lowercase)#
abcdefghijklmnopqrstuvwxyz
print(string.ascii_uppercase)#
ABCDEFGHIJKLMNOPQRSTUVWXYZ
print(string.ascii_letters)#
abcdefghijklmnopqrstuvwxyzABCDEFGHIJK#
LMNOPQRSTUVWXYZ

print(string.digits) #0123456789

print(string. punctuation)   #!"#$%&'()*+,-
./:;<=>?@[\]^_`{|}~

Output[36]:   abcdefghijklmnopqrstuvwxyz
ABCDEFGHIJKLMNOPQRSTUVWXYZ

abcdefghijklmnopqrstuvwxyzABCDEFGHIJKL
MNOPQRSTUVWXYZ 0123456789

 !"#$%&'()*+,-./:;<=>?@[\]^_`{|}~

Text Files: File Handle

From now on, we will start working with databases in text format. To do so, we will need to make use of the open() function, which allows the opening of text files for reading and writing (writing) of files. But what does it mean to open a file? This question is undoubtedly a rather important one! So you deserve a detailed answer.

As data scientists, we know that working with archives will be one of our main routines. Every time a Python program needs to access a file - either to import it entirely into memory or to process it sequentially (line by line) - it is necessary, first of all, to use the open() function to command its opening.

Internally (in those "mysterious" processes that happen inside the computer), the open() function establishes a "conversation" between Python and the computer operating system (Windows, Mac, Linux). Better explaining: opening a file means asking the operating system to find the location address of the file on the hard drive, flash drive, SD card, or the device on which it is stored.

When it finds the file address, the operating system will return something called a filehandle to the Python program. The filehandle is not the same as the content of the file, i.e., it does not consist of the actual data. Actually, it is a kind of tool that allows you to "handle" the data in the file.

In the following lessons, we will show you how to use the "basic mode" offered by Python and its standard library to work with text files. But first of all, it is very important to make it clear that there are libraries that offer much more practical ways to work with text databases, especially structured files in CSV format. An example of the 'pandas' library will be presented inside the very beginning of the next Data Science With Python Book.

Anyway, we consider it important that you first know and learn how to use Python's standard way of handling files for two reasons:

(i)   the filehandle based technique is often the most efficient alternative for performing sequential access to files, a process where only one line at a time is loaded into memory. In many real applications, where the database to be worked on is very large and does not fit in memory, sequential access ends up being even the only possible method of access;

(ii)   the filehandle is simple and suitable to handle files separated by columns. Although this format is not very popular today, it is still used in some applications (for example, it is adopted by many countries to store demographic census data).

Text Files: Processing Column Separated File

Program 37 - Reading of File Separated by Columns - Fixed Size

The file "ARQ_COLUNAS.txt," presented below, stores information of two variables: "n1", a numeric variable, which starts in column 1 and has a fixed size of 4 columns; and "c1", a character type variable, starting in column 5 and with a fixed size of 5 columns.

    1001 aaaaaa

    1002 bbbbb

    1003 ccccc

    1004 ddddd

    1005 eeeeeee

Suppose this file is stored in the "C:\CursoPython" folder (we'll use this assumption for all examples from now on – change the code if you are using another folder). Next, it shows a program that opens the file, reads it line by line (sequential access) and captures the two variables.

    #

    P037: read file separated by columns

    nameArq = 'C:
    /PythonCourse/ARQ_COLUMNS.txt'

f = open(nameArq)

is line in f:

n1 = line[: 4] c1 = line[4:] print(n1, c1)

Output[37]:

1001 yyyyyy

1002 bbbbb

1003 ccccccc

1004 ddddddd

1005 eeeeeee

The following is an explanation of how the program works. Initially, the open() function is used to open the file, whose path is stored in the string variable "nameArq." The "f" variable, which gets the result returned by the open() function, does not store the file itself. Instead, it stores a filehandle returned by the operating system, which represents a kind of "pointer" to the real file (points to the file address). Therefore, if you have "f" printed, you will not see the contents of the file on the screen, but rather a "weird text" that describes the filehandle.

The command for line in f: allows the file pointed by "f" to be swept from the first to the last line. In other words, this command implements sequential access to the file. In this technique, the file is not imported into memory.

On the contrary, each iteration of the is, only one line is loaded into memory, and its contents have been copied to the "line" variable.

Within each iteration, the command n1 = line[:4] causes the substring formed by the first 4 characters of "line" to be stored in the variable "n1". Remember that the first character of a string always has the index 0 - so the command presented captures the index characters 0, 1, 2, and 3. Similarly, c1 = line[4:] copies to "c1" the substring that begins with index 4 and goes to the last character of "line."

When running the example, you should have noticed that a blank line was printed between each result produced by print(n1, c1). This occurred because the last character of a read line from the file is actually the "\n" character (it is invisible to us, but exists in the file!). To avoid printing "\n" (the guy that generates a blank line), just make the following modification in the program:

```
c1 = line[4:9]
```

This way, "c1" will receive the substring between the fourth and the eighth character of the variable "line" (don't forget that the slicing always goes from the first index to the last minus one).

Another important thing to mention is that in sequential access, we can only "move forward" in the file. Once a line is reached, there is no way back to the previous line unless you close and open the file again, and implement another command to scan the file to the desired line.

Program 38 - Reading of Separate File by Columns - Variable Size

Now consider the file "PRODUTOS.txt," which contains the code and name of some products. Although it is a file separated by columns, it is different from the file shown in the previous subsection, because the length of each one of its rows is variable (the names of each product have different lengths).

> 1001Lite
>
> 1002Biscuit
>
> 1003Caffé
>
> 1004Rates
>
> 1005Tea

For the file to be processed correctly, the mallet is to use the len() function, which returns the length of a string (beware, because this size includes the annoying "\n," since we are dealing with file lines).

> \#
>
> P038: read file separated by columns - variable size
>
> nameArq = 'C:/CursoPython/PRODUTOS.txt'

```
f = open(nameArq)


is line in f:

  code = line[: 4]

name = line[4: len(line) - 1]

print(code, name)


Output[40]:

  1001 Milk

1002 Biscuit

1003 Coffee

1004 Toast

1005 Tea
```

Text Files: Importing an Entire File into a String

If you are working with a not too large file, you can import it entirely into memory using the read() method, which is offered by the filehandle object (yes, yes, the filehandle is a Python object!). When a file is read this way, all its characters (including all the shameless "\n"! characters) are stored in a single "string," as the

145

following example shows. Obviously, this process cannot be performed for very large files.

Program 39 - Reading an Entire File to a String

```
#

P039: Import whole file into a string

nameArq = 'C: /CoursePython/PRODUCTS.txt'

f = open(nameArq)

content = f.read()

print(content)
```

Output[39]:

1001 Lite

1002 Cookie

1003 Coffee

1004 Rates

1005 Tea

Text Files: Processing CSV files

We can also read CSV files (comma-separated values) and other types of files based on delimiting characters using standard Python, as we will see in the following examples.

Program 40 - Reading of CSV File - Basic Process

The "CEPS.csv" file stores information about ranges of CEPs used in states in the Southeast region. The first value corresponds to the initial CEP, the second to the final CEP, and the last to the UF name. The first line of the file contains the header, that is, the description of the variables.

zip_ini, zip_ep ,uf_name

20000000.28999999, Colorado

29000000,29999999, California

30000000,39999999, New York

01000000,19999999, New Jersey

To read this CSV file separating the variables correctly, we can use the split() method, available automatically for any variable of type string. This method breaks a string in a word list by simply passing the delimiter character as a parameter. An example is given in the following code, which opens the "CEPS.csv" file for sequential access, "skips" the header line, and prints the initial and final zip code for each FU.

#

P040: file reading separated by the delimiter

147

```python
nameArq = 'C:/CursoPython/CEPS.csv'

f = open(nameeArq)


aux = 0# auxiliary to allow header to be ignored

is line in f:

    if (aux > 0): #ignorates the header line

    line = line[: len(line) - 1]# Remove the
    tremendously annoying "\n"

    lstWords = line.split(",") cep_ini = lstWords[0]
    cep_fim = lstWords[1]


    uf = lstWords[2]

    print(uf + " -> CEPS from " + cep_ini + " a " +
    cep_fim) aux = aux + 1
```

Output[40]:
```
Colorado - > CEPS from 20000000 to 28999999
California - > CEPS from 29000000 to 29999999
New York - > CEPS from New York to 39999999
New jersey - > CEPS from 01000000 to 19999999
```

148

Program 41 - Conversion of Types

The file "EMPLOYEES.csv," presented below, has the name, age, and salary of the employees of a hypothetical company.

Jane;55;2500.00

Gregory;32;1200.50

Rakesh;48;4999.99

Mia;29;1900.00

Pete;50;2900.00

Consider that the company wishes to give a premium equivalent to 15% of the salary to all employees aged 50 or over. To create a program that identifies such employees and determines the amount of the bonus to be paid to each of them, it is necessary not only to read each line of the file, separating the information three distinct variables, "name," "age" and "salary."

It is also necessary to specify which variable "age" is of the int type (since we will need to make a comparison involving age) and "salary" of the float type (because we will need to make a calculation based on the value of the salary). As we saw in Chapter II, the Python language offers predefined functions for type conversion that can be used in situations like this:

- int(x): converts "x" to an int, where "x" can be a string or a float;

- float(x): converts "x" to a float, where "x" can be a string or an int.

- str(x): convert "x" to a string, where "x" can be an int or a float.

The following code solves the proposed problem. Analyze it carefully:

```
#

P041: CSV file reading and type conversion

nameArq = 'C:/CursoPython/EMPLOYEES.csv'

f = open(nameArq)


is line in f:

  line = line[: len(line) - 1]# Remove the "/n"

annoyance

lstAux = line.split(";") name = lstAux[0]

age = int(lstAux[1]) salary = float(lstAux[2]) if
(age > 49):

  premium = salary * 0.15

print(name + " -> won a prize of $ " + str(prize))
```

Output[41]:

```
    Jane - > won a prize of $ 375.0 Pete -
> won a prize of $ 435.0
```

Text Files: Recording Files

To save a file, you must open it using the "w" mode as the second parameter of the open() function. When recording is finished, you must use the close() function to close the file.

Program 42 - Recording of Text Files

#

P042 - Saving a text file

fout = open('C: / Python_Course / fragile_touch.txt', 'w') msg1 = "The smile \ n"

msg2 = "Do \ n"

msg3 = "Puppy"

msg4 = "Okay"

msg5 = "In the ass ... \ n"

fout write("Touch Fragile (Walter Franco) \ n")
fout.write("===========================")

fout write("\ n")

151

```
fout write(msg1 + msg2 + msg3 + msg4 +
msg5) fout.close()
```

After the execution, the program will have generated a file with six lines, called "toque_fragil.txt" in the folder "C:\PythonCourse."

Text Files: Knowing the Unicode Standard

What is Unicode?

Unicode is a globally adopted standard that enables all characters of all the written languages used on the planet can be represented on computers. A Unicode's mission is clearly presented on the Unicode Consortium web site (the entity responsible for its management):

Unicode provides a unique number for each character,

> *no matter the platform,*

> *no matter the program,*

> *no matter the language.*

The Unicode standard represents not only the letters used by the languages familiar to Westerners, such as English, Spanish, French, and Portuguese but also letters and symbols used in any other language - Russian, Japanese, Chinese, Hebrew, etc. In addition, it includes punctuation symbols, technical symbols and other characters that can be used in written text.

How Does Unicode Work?

In Unicode, each different letter or symbol of each alphabet used in the world is mapped to a different code point. The code point is a code in U format + number in hexadecimal. The example below shows the codes of the letters that make up the word "BRAZIL" (in capital letters).

B - U+0042

R - U+0052

A - U+0041

S - U+0053

I - U+0049

L - U+004C

It is very important to mention that uppercase letters have different code points than lowercase letters. For example, the code point of the letter "A" is U+0041, while that of the letter "a" is U+0061. The code point of "Ç" is U+00C7, and that of "ç" is U+00E7 (and so on). Another important observation is that the first 127 code points (up to U+007F) are compatible with the codes used in the old ASCII table, the first one created to standardize character encoding.

These 127 code points basically represent the codes associated with the most common numbers, uppercase, and lowercase letters without accent and punctuation symbols.

The Windows Character Map (charmap) application can be used to query the Unicode table. To access it, just go to the Command Prompt and type charmap. In Figure 14, the Character Map shows the code point associated with the capital letter Á ("A" with an acute accent).

Encodings

From what has been presented so far, we can understand that Unicode is nothing more than a huge table that associates a unique number (code point) to each different letter or symbol of the alphabets around the world. But how can these code points be stored in a text file or in computer memory? That's where the encodings come in.

An encoding is a scheme for storing the code points of the characters that make up the strings in computer memory. There are several of them: UTF-8, ISO-8859-1 (dubbed Latin-1), UCS-2, ANSI (or Windows-1252), etc.

Each encoding uses a distinct technique to handle Unicode codes. The UTF-8 encoding, for example, is capable of representing any Unicode character. To achieve this, it uses a technique where a quantity of 1 to 6 bytes can be used to represent each character.

That is, UTF-8 does not work with a fixed-size representation. Code points from 0 to 127 are stored with 1 byte. However, the others can be stored in memory with a size of 2 to 6 bytes. UTF-8 is complete (stores any Unicode character) and uses a storage technique that can be considered "sophisticated."

Other encodings, such as ISO-8859-1 and ANSI, are less complete than UTF-8, and prefer to work with only a subset of the Unicode table (e.g., Western language characters only). On the other hand, they can make use of simpler storage techniques that, in addition, can represent strings spending a smaller number of bytes.

But, why is it so important for a data scientist to know what Unicode is? What encoding, UTF-8 standard, Latin-1 standard, ANSI standard, etc., is? It is because, in many practical situations, it becomes necessary to warn Python (in fact, any programming language) the encoding of a file so that it is possible to open it.

Better detailing - if a file contains only conventional characters, such as code points from 0 to 127, i.e., letters without accent, numbers, most common punctuation marks, tab, blank space, "\n," etc., its encoding doesn't matter; all encodings use the same internal scheme to store them.

But if the file contains some special character, even if it is an innocent cedilla or an accented letter, "a" Python will not be able to process it if you don't enter the correct encoding. This is because the different encodings use different techniques to store special characters. You'll see this in detail in the 'Text files: UTF-8 versus ANSI' Lesson!

Text files: 'csv' module

In 'Processing CSV Files Lesson,' we showed that it is possible to access CSV files using the open() function in conjunction with the split() string method. However, the standard library offers the 'csv' module, which has the interesting ability to associate lines of CSV files with lists and dictionaries.

Program 43 - Module 'csv' in List Mode

The use of the 'csv' module will be demonstrated through examples that use the file "PAISES.csv"20. This file stores a small database with 10 observations and 5 variables: country acronym, country name, continent ('A'=America or 'E'=Europe), territorial extension (in km2) and population size.

abbreviation;name;continent;extension;population

BRA;Brazil;A;8515767;204450649

CUB;Cuba;A;109890;11389562

FRA;France;E;549190;64395345

HUN;Hungary;E;93030;9855023

ITA;Italy;E;301340;59797685

MEX;Mexico;A;1964380;127017224

NOR;Norway;E;323780;5210967

PER;Peru;A;1285220;31376670

PRT;Portugal;E;92090;10349803

URY;Uruguay;A;176220;3431555

#

P043: working with the "csv"

module in LIST mode

```python
import csv


with open('C:/CursoPython/paises.csv', 'rt') as f:
    meu_csv = csv.reader(f, delimiter = ';')

    for line in my_csv:

        print(line)
```

Output[43]: ['acronym', 'name', 'continent', 'extension', 'population']
```
    ['BRA', 'Brazil', 'A', '8515767',
    '204450649']
    ['CUB', 'Cuba', 'A', '109890',
    '11389562']
    ['FRA', 'France', 'E', '549190',
    '64395345']
    ['HUN', 'Hungary', 'E', '93030',
    '9855023']
```

```
  ['ITA', 'Italy', 'E', '301340',
'59797685']
  ['MEX', 'Mexico', 'A', '1964380',
'127017224']
  ['NOR', 'Norway', 'E', '323780',
'5210967']
  ['PER', 'Peru', 'A', '1285220',
'31376670']
  ['PRT', 'Portugal', 'E', '92090',
'10349803']
  ['URY', 'Uruguay', 'A', '176220',
'3431555']
```

The program has only 5 lines, which are explained below:

- import csv

   o Import the 'csv' module.

- with open ('C: /PythonCourse/paises.csv', 'rt') as f:

   o Opens the file for reading ('rt' parameter), associating it with the file handle "f".

- my_csv = csv.reader (f, delimiter = ';')

   o Creates the "my_csv" object, of type csv.reader. This type of object understands what a CSV file is and allows iteration over its lines. Notice that two parameters have been passed: the file handle ("f") and the delimiter (";").

- for line in my_csv:

print (line)

  o Scans the entire CSV file sequentially, from first to last line.

Program 44 - Choosing the Variables of Interest

Using the "csv" package, each line of the file is loaded as a list instead of a string. This greatly facilitates the processing of the file, because each variable is associated with a specific index. In our example, "acronym" stands for index 0, "name" for index 1, etc., as shown in the program below, which only prints the acronym and the population of each country, and does not print the header.

```
#

P044: Reads CSV and prints only 2 variables

import csv

with open('C:/CursoPython/paises.csv', 'rt') as f:
meu_csv = csv.reader(f, delimiter = ';')

i = 0;

for line in my_csv:
```

        if i > 0: #to ignore the header

        print(line[0] + ' -> population = ' + line[4]) i = i
        + 1

Output[44]:

```
BRA - > population = 204450649 CUB - >
population = 11389562 FRA - > population
= 64395345 HUN - > population = 9855023
ITA - > population = 59797685 MEX - >
population = 127017224 NOR - >
population = 5210967 PER - > population
= 31376670 PRT - > population = 10349803
URY - > population = 3431555
```

Program 45 - Module 'csv' in Dictionary Mode

Using the DictReader() method, you can structure each
line of a CSV file in a dictionary instead of a list. With
the use of this module:

(i)   the header row is automatically interpreted
        and imported;

(ii)   each variable can be referenced by its name
        and not by its position.

        #

        P045: Reading a CSV file as a dictionary

        import csv

160

```
with open('C:/CursoPython/paises.csv', 'rt') as f:
meu_csv = csv.DictReader(f, delimiter = ';') for
linha in meu_csv:
```

```
  print(line["acronym"] + ' -> population = ' +
line["population"])
```

Output[45]:

```
BRA - > population = 204450649 CUB - >
population = 11389562 FRA - > population
= 64395345 HUN - > population = 9855023
ITA - > population = 59797685 MEX - >
population = 127017224 NOR - >
population = 5210967 PER - > population
= 31376670 PRT - > population = 10349803
URY - > population = 3431555
```

'csv' Module

- The 'csv' module offers several other advanced functionalities for the interpretation of CSV files (e.g., dialects, formatting parameters, etc.). However, as our book is introductory, we prefer to show only the "cake recipe."

- Additionally, it is important to mention that in later chapters, we will show how the 'NumPy' and 'pandas' libraries can be used to import CSV files directly to vectors, matrices, and DataFrames in memory.

161

Text Files: UTF-8 Versus ANSI

As previously introduced in Lesson 'Text files: csv 'Module,' encodings often give a lot of headaches to non-informats who are developing scripts in Python, R, and other languages. Remember, an encoding consists of a scheme used for storing character codes. Different encodings, such as UTF-8 and ANSI, use different storage techniques and, for this reason, when working with a text file in a Python program, it is important to identify its encoding so that no error occurs in the program's processing.

Program 46 - File with UTF-8 Encoding (opening the wrong way)

Suppose the file "ARTICLES.csv", listed below, was saved with UTF-8 encoding. See that, apparently, it has no difference from any other file:

> player,goals
>
> Helium,20
>
> Andrey,15
>
> John, 12
>
> Antonio,11

However, if you try to open this file with the open() command without specifying the UTF-8 encoding, an error may occur or, worse, your program may generate "crazy" results, as the example below shows:

\#

P046: PROBLEM when opening file in utf - 8 encoding

import csv

with open('C: /PythonCourse / SHARES.csv', 'rt') as f: my_csv = csv.reader(f, delimiter = ',')

for line in my_csv:

  print(line[0] + '->' + line[1])

Output[46]:

```
    ï "¿player -> goals Helium -> 20
Andrey - > 15
John - > 12
Antonio - > 11
```

Please note that the accented characters in the names have not been printed correctly, and some strange symbols have appeared before the word "player." Luckily, fixing the problem is simple: the encoding parameter should be used in the open() command to indicate that the file is encoded in the "utf-8" format.

Program 47 - File with UTF-8 Encoding (opening the right way)

\#

P047: CERTAIN way to open file in utf - 8 encoding

```
import csv

with open('C: /PythonCourse/TARKS.csv', 'rt',
encoding = "utf-8") as f: my_csv = csv.reader(f,
delimiter = ',')

for line in my_csv:

print(line[0] + '->' + line[1])
```

Output[47]:
```
player - > helium goals - > 20
Andrey - > 15
John - > 12
Antonio - > 11
```

But you might be wondering: how do I find out how to
encode a text file? A simple way to check is the
following: open the file with NOTEPAD and then
choose the option Save As. In the window that will
open. If it says "UTF-8", you need to use the parameter
encoding="utf-8"; if it says "ANSI" you don't need it.
After checking, just click the Cancel button.

Text Files: Processing JSON Files

JSON (JavaScript Object Notation) is a template for
storing and transmitting information in text format.
Although very simple, it is the most used by Web
applications due to its ability to structure information in
a much more compact way than that achieved by its
biggest rival, the XML model, making faster the parsing
(processing and interpretation) of this information. This

explains why JSON has been adopted by companies such as Google and Yahoo, whose applications need to transmit large volumes of data.

Syntax

The idea used by JSON to represent information is tremendously simple: for each value represented, a name (or label) is assigned that describes its meaning. This syntax is derived from the way the JavaScript language represents information. For example, to represent the year 2019, the following syntax is used:

"year": 2019

You probably noticed that the syntax is very similar to the one used by the ED dictionary, discussed in the previous chapter: we have a key mapped to a value. A name:value pair should be represented by the name in double quotation marks, followed by a colon, followed by the value. Values can have only three basic types: numeric (integer or real), boolean (true or false, lowercase), and string. There is also a null value to represent missing information.

The following are some examples of information represented in JSON. Note that values of type string must be enclosed in quotation marks (as in dictionaries!)

"first name": "Jane": "Last name": "Austen": "Age": 41

"9.9 "approved": true

From the basic types, it is possible to build complex types: array and object. Arrays are enclosed in square brackets, with their elements separated by commas. Below is an example of an array of strings:

("RJ","SP","MG","ES")

Now an example of JSON representation for an integer array (actually, the identity array of order 3).

[[1,0,0],

[0,1,0],

[0,0,1]]

Objects are specified between keys and can consist of multiple names:value pairs, arrays, and also other objects. In this way, a JSON object can represent virtually any type of information! The example below shows how we can use JSON to represent data from a movie.

{

"title": "JSON x CSV."

"summary": "the duel between two formats to represent information", "year": 2019,

"gender." ["adventure", "action", "fiction"]

}

You can represent more than one object or record at a time by simply doing so

use an array. In the example below, the way to represent two films in JSON is shown:

```
[
{
"title": "JSON x CSV."

"summary": "the duel between two formats to represent information", "year": 2019,

"gender." ["adventure", "action", "fiction"]
},
{
"title": "JSON James."

"summary": "the story of a legend of the Old West", "year": 2018,

"gender." ["western"]
}
]
```

Program 48 - Importing JSON Files

In the following program, we will use the 'json' module (plus a standard library module) to process the 'cinema.json' file. Consider that the contents of the file are identical to the example we just presented, containing the information of the movies "JSON x CSV" and "JSON James."

```
#

P048: Importing a JSON file

import json


#(1) - Imports JSON file to memory nameArq
= 'C: /CoursePython/cinema.json'

with open(nameArq) as f:

  movies = json.load(f)


#(2) - Processes each film sequentially

print('')

print('Type of variable'

  films ':', type(films)) print('Total films =',
len(films))


for film in movies:

  print('')
```

168

print('Type of variable'

  film ':', type(film)) print('Title:', film['title'])

print('Abstract:', film['abstract'])

print('Year:', movie['year'])

print('Genre (s):', film['genre'])

Output[48]:

```
 -- -- -- -- -- -- -- -- -- -- -- -- --
-- -- -- -- -- -- --
Type of variable "films": < class 'list'
> Total films = 2
 -- -- -- -- -- -- -- -- -- -- -- -- --
-- -- -- -- -- -- --
Type of variable "film": < class 'dict'
> Title: JSON x CSV
Summary: The duel between two formats to
represent information Year: 2019
Gender(s): ['adventure', 'action',
'fiction']
 -- -- -- -- -- -- -- -- -- -- -- -- --
-- -- -- -- -- -- --
Type of variable "film": < class 'dict'
> Title: JSON James
Summary: The Story of a Legend of the
Old West Year: 2018
Gender(s): ['western']
```

The program is divided into two parts:

- In the first part, we have the "cake recipe" for reading JSON files: we use the load() method that, when called, loads the entire file into memory, structuring it in a list of dictionaries. See how interesting: the file "cinema.json" (file containing two films) was entirely imported to a list in which each element (film) is a dictionary. The dictionary has 4 keys: "title" (string), "abstract" (string), "year" (int) and "generous" (list). This demonstrates the flexibility of the JSON (and Python) format to represent complex information in a very natural way.

- In the second part, we use them for the command to iterate over our list of movies. With each iteration, a movie is retrieved, and its properties can be displayed using normal syntax to index dictionaries (shown in the Dictionaries Lesson).

- An important comment: by default, the 'json' module assumes that the file has the

- ANSI encoding.

Program 49 - Recording JSON Files

The following is a program that writes the contents of a list of dictionaries to a JSON file using the dump() method.

```
#

P049: Recording a JSON file
```

```python
import json


#(1) - Creates the list of dictionaries

movies = []


movies.append({

  "title": "Noel, Poet of the Village.

  summary ':'

  The film tells the story of composer Noel Rosa
','

  year ': 2006,

  ...gender: ['Biography', 'Musical']

})


movies.append({

  'title': 'Edukators',

  summary ':'

  In a creative way,

  two young people fight against the system ','
```

```python
    year ': 2004,
    ...gender: ['Action', 'Drama', 'Thriller']
})


movies.append({
    "Title": "A Chinese Story.
    summary ':'
    grumpy Argentinian decides to help desperate
Chinese ','
    year ': 2011,
    ...gender: ['Comedy', 'Drama']
})


#(2) - Export the data to a file
nameArq = 'C: /PythonCourse/tres_movies.json'.


with open(filename, 'w') as f_exit:
json.dump(movies, f_exit, ensure_ascii = False)


print('Successfully saved file ...')
```

Output[49]:

```
        File successfully recorded...
```

Final Comments

In this lesson, we only discuss "beans with rice" on the subject. Some important, but slightly more "dense" topics about JSON have been left out, e.g., serialization and deserialization. To close, a summary of the main features of the JSON format:

- Used to represent information in text format;

- It has a self-descriptive nature (i.e., it is enough to "hit the eye" on a JSON file to understand its meaning);

- It is able to represent in a simple and natural way complex information. Some examples: composite objects (objects within objects), hierarchy relationships, arrays, missing data, and so on. This type of information is very difficult to represent in tabular format;

- It is a de facto standard for data representation: it was formalized in RFC 4627.

- It is independent of programming language. Data represented in JSON can be accessed by any programming language, through specific libraries (in the case of Python, we use the 'json' module of the standard library).

Regular Expressions

A regular expression (regexp) can be defined as a rule that specifies a particular pattern to be searched for in a text. Not only Python but almost all modern programming languages, in addition to most text editors, offer this tool to their users.

Although the regular expressions are very powerful, they are a bit complicated. It wouldn't be an exaggeration to say that they are almost a programming language (it doesn't get that much more is quaaaase). No doubt, it takes some time for a person to get the hang of it and become fluent in reading and writing regexps!

But it's worth studying because it's a technique widely used in text mining, web scraping, and other data science tasks related to the analysis of text documents. There are whole books that deal with regexps, and in this lesson, we'll introduce just a "little taste" of the topic, so you can at least "get out of the woods."

Before we begin, one thing is clear: the 're' module needs to be imported into your program so that you can work with regular expressions. That is, you will have to put the command below in your program:

import re

Search() function

The 're' module has a good number of functions23, being search() the best known. As its own name indicates, it searches for a pattern in a text and returns True if it is found (False, otherwise).

Program 50 - Regexp - Search() Function

Consider the text file "dez_filmes.txt," which, as the name indicates, stores information about ten different movies:

> Run, Lola, Run (1998) | Action, Adventure, Thriller Educators (2004) | Action, Drama, Thriller
>
> The Belier Family (2014) | Comedy, Drama The Son of the Bride
>
> Hair (1979) | Drama, War, Musical Jane Eyre (1943) | Drama, Romance
>
> La La Land | Comedy, Musical, Romance
>
> Nise: The Heart of Madness (2015) | Biography, History The Bridges of Madison | Drama, Romance
>
> Noel - Poet of the Village | Biography, Music

You will get the file's a little messy. It is not exactly a CSV, much less JSON, nor is it separated by columns. But in a way, it has some pattern. First, note that each line refers to a different film. Some of the films have a title, year of production in parentheses, then the delimiter "|" followed by a list of genres. Others have only the title, the "|" separator, and the genres. There is still a single film without the information of the year and the genres ("The Son of the Bride").

In the example below, a program is presented in which it opens the file "dez_filmes.txt" and throws all its content into a string variable called "content." This string is then "broken" into a list (each line of the file becomes an element of the list). Finally, a loop is made over the list, and search() is used to identify and print only the lines that contain the word 'Musical.'

```
#

P050 Regexp basicone

import re



#(1) - Imports the entire file to a string and then
converts it to a list#(each line of the file
becomes an element of the list)

nameArq = 'C: /PythonCourse/dez_filmes.txt'

f = open(nameArq)

content = f.read()

lst_films = content.split("\ n")



#(2) - Use search() to find the lines that have the
word "Musical"
```

```
for line in lst_films:

    if re.search('Musical', line):

    print(line)
```

Output[50]:

Hair(1979) | Drama, War, Musical

La La Land | Comedy, Musical, Romance Noel -
Poet of the Village | Biography, Musical

Metacharacters

The previous example does not demonstrate by far the true power of regular expressions, because we could have solved the same problem by simply using the find() method, available for string type variables (see 'String' Lesson). In fact, when we work with regexps, it's cool even from the moment we define rules that use metacharacters.

Metacharacters are special symbols that have specific functions and can be combined to generate complex expressions. They can be classified into four distinct types: anchors, representatives, quantifiers, and others. The metacharacters belonging to each category are presented, explained, and exemplified consequently below.

Anchor-Type Metacharacters

Purpose: they serve to select specific positions in a row

^   It marks the beginning of a line.

- ^A' : get lines starting with the letter "A" (upper case).

$ It marks the end of a line.

- "Drama$": you get lines that end with "Drama.

Metacharacters of Type Representative

Purpose: Used to represent one or more characters

.   Represents any character (wildcard)

- 19.3': marries '1943', '1983', '1903', '19A3', '19Z3', etc.

- "B.la": marries "Bela", "Bala", "Bola", etc.

- Com.dia': marries 'Comedy', 'Comedia', 'Comxdia', 'Com1dia', etc.

[...]   Represents a list of allowed characters.

- "Dd]rama": marries only "drama" and "drama.

- 201[123]' : matches only '2011', '2012', '2013'.

- "<[Bb]>" : matches only "<B>" and <b>.

[^...] Represents a list of characters not allowed.

- ^Dd]rama' : Never marry 'Drama' or 'drama' (but you could marry 'Trama,' for example).

Metacharacters of Type Quantifier

Purpose: they serve to indicate the number of repetitions allowed for a given pattern, which should be specified to the left of the metacharacter.

?   Zero or a repeat.

- 'Eyr?e' : marries 'Eye' and 'Eyre.'

- "Ii]phone[45]? marries 'Iphone', 'iphone', 'Iphone4', 'iphone4', 'Iphone5' and 'iphone5'.

*   Zero, one or more repetitions.

- Dra*ma': marries 'Drma', 'Drama', 'Draama', 'Draaama', etc.

- 2*0': box with '0', '20', '220', '2220', etc.

+   One or more repetitions.

- Dra+ma': marries 'Drama', 'Draama', 'Draaama', etc.

- 2+0' : house with '20', '220', '2220', etc.

??? Minimum n and maximum m repetitions.

- dr[a]{2,3}ma' : marries only 'draama' and 'draaama'.

Other Meta Characteristics

| Used when we want to specify alternatives (or).

- 2004 | 2014': matches with '2004' or 2014'.

- [Dd] rama | [Rr] omance | [Cc] omedy': marries 'Drama', 'drama', 'Romance', 'romance', 'comedy' or 'comedy'.

() Used to group characters or metacharacters, allowing the specification of regexps more complex (group).

- 'A (n | m) (e | a)': marries 'Ana', 'Ane', 'Ama' and 'Ame'.

\ Called "escape" is used to indicate that a particular symbol used as a metacharacter, such as "|", ".", "^," "$," etc., should be treated as a normal character (exhaust).

180

- '\ | Comedy': marries '| Comedy'.

\ s   Blank space

- '\ sDrama': Matches only 'Drama' (whitespace + 'Drama').

\ S   Anything other than a whitespace

'\ S   Anything that's not a blank space

- Drama': Never marries 'Drama' (white space + 'Drama'), but marries "| Drama", for example.

Intervals

[A-Z]   List with the letters without accent (in capital letters);

[a-z]   List with the letters without accent (in lowercase);

[A-Za-z]   List of all non-accented letters, regardless of whether they are in upper or lower case;

[0-9]   Digits from 0 to 9.

The great power of regular expressions lies in the possibility of combining all these features into a single rule, as the following program shows.

Program 51 - Regexps with Metacharacters and Intervals

The program below presents several examples of regular expressions that use metacharacters to search for very specific patterns in the movie database.

```
#

P051 Regexps with metacharacters

import re


#(1) - Imports the entire file to a string and then
converts it to a list#(each line of the file
becomes an element of the list)

nameArq = 'C: /PythonCourse/dez_filmes.txt'

f = open(nameArq)

content = f.read()

lst_films = content.split("\ n")


#(2 a) - Find the movies that start with "O" +
space or "A" + space

print('')

print('* * * Movies beginning with "O" + space
or "A" + space')
```

```python
for line in lst_films:

  if re.search('^ (O | A) \ s', line):

  print(line)


#(2 b) - Find the films that have a registered year

print('n') print('* * * Films with year registered')


for line in lst_films:

  if re.search('\ ([0-9] + \)', line):

  print(line)


#? (2 c) - Find the movies that have some words with "a."

and then "r".#(regardless of the number of letters between "a."

  and "r")


print('n')

print('* * * Movies with words that have "a" and then "r")
```

```
for line in lst_films:

    if re.search('[A-Za-z] * to [A-Za-z] * r', row):

        print(line)
```

Output[51]:

-- --

*

* Movies beginning with "O" + space or "A"
+ space The Bélier Family(2014) | Comedy,
Drama The Son of the Bride | Comedy, Drama

-- --

*

* Films with registered year Run, Lola,
Run(1998) | Action, Adventure, Thriller
Edukators(2004) | Action, Drama, Thriller The
Belier Family(2014) | Comedy, Drama
Hair(1979) | Drama, War, Musical Jane
Eyre(1943) | Drama, Romance Nise: The Heart
of Madness(2015) | Biography, History

-- --

*

* Films with words that have "a"

184
```
```

and then "r"

Educators(2004) | Action, Drama, Thriller
Hair(1979) | Drama, War, Musical

Explanation

- The regular expression '^(O|A)\s' matches any line that starts with the letter 'O' or the letter 'A' and then has a blank space. See that there is a film that starts with "As," and that was left out ("The Bridges of Madison") because we just wanted to start with "O"+space or "A"+space.

- The regular expression '\([0-9]+\)' matches any line that has an open parenthesis (see that you need to use the escape "\" because the parenthesis is a metacharacter), then a sequence with or more numbers and then a closed parenthesis (again "escaped" with "\"). With this, regexp can recover the films that have the year informed.

- Finally, the complicated regular expression '[A-Za-z]*a[A-Za-z]*r' matches any line starting with zero or more uppercase or lowercase letters ([A-Za-z]*), then has the letter "a" lowercase, zero or more uppercase or lowercase letters ([A-Za-z]*) and then has the letter "r" lowercase!

Findall() Function

The findall(r,s) function is used to extract all substrings of a string s that match the regexp specified in r. The function returns a list containing all identified substrings (if none is found, it returns an empty list). That is: this function not only serves to find patterns in a text but also to extract them.

Program 52 - Findall() Function

One of the most widely used approaches in text mining applications is the so-called bag of words. In this approach, each word in a corpus (set of documents) is transformed into a variable. The code below shows how the findall() function can be used to identify and extract all the words present in the titles of each film. All scores will be discarded, keeping only the letters.

```
#

P052 Regexp with findall()

import re


   #(1) - Imports the entire file to a string and then
converts it to a list#(each line of the file
becomes an element of the list)

nameArq = 'C: /PythonCourse/dez_filmes.txt'

f = open(nameArq)
```

```
content = f.read()

lst_films = content.split("\n")
```

```
#(2) - Transform each movie title into a "word
bag"#
```

```
print('') print('* * * words in each film title:')
```

```
for line in lst_films:
```

```
    title = line.split("|")[0]# Hold only the title,
    discarding    the    genera    bag_words    =
    re.findall('[A-Za-záéíóúúâêôôõçç]    +',    title)
    print(bag_words)
```

Output[52]:

```
-- -- -- -- -- -- -- -- -- -- -- -- -- -- -- -- -- -- -- --

*

* words in every movie title: ['Run', 'Lola',
'Run']['Edukators']

['A', 'Family', 'Bélier']

['O', 'Son', 'da', 'Bride']['Hair']

['Jane', 'Eyre']['La', 'La', 'Land']

['Nise', 'O', 'Heart', 'da', 'Madness']
```

['As', 'Bridges', 'From', 'Madison']

['Noel', 'Poet', 'da', 'Village']

In this program, inside the for loop, the title of the movie from its genres using the split() method was separated first. Then, we make the variable "wordbag" receive the result of the findall() function applied over the title and using the regexp '[A-Za-záéíóúúâêôõõçç]+.' This regexp specifies that we want to find all the sequences formed by one or more letters among those specified in the list between brackets. As a result, for each title, the program generates a list with the sequences found (which actually form a word).

Well, let's finish up this chapter here. As mentioned at the beginning of the lesson, regular expressions are not a trivial subject, and our aim here was only to give a presentation on the subject. To become an expert in regexps, you will need to study some book entirely dedicated to the subject.

Chapter Six

SQL Database and Language

Although most of the digital information is available in text format (HTML, CSV, JSON, Word, etc.), it is very important to take into account that "most" does not mean "everything"! There is a large volume of relevant data that is not structured in text files, but rather in tables of relational databases such as Oracle, MySQL, and Microsoft SQL Server.

This is the typical case of data collected and produced by corporate systems - applications developed for essentially business needs, such as HR system, collections system, product catalog, supplier system, inventory control, academic system, sales system, etc..

The data stored in relational databases must be consulted and updated using a language specially developed for this purpose, called SQL. This is basically the only language that relational banks understand! Therefore, it is important for every data scientist to learn a little SQL and how to access relational databases within Python programs.

In this chapter, we provide a brief introduction to these matters. You will notice that the text is centered on a single (but beautiful) SQL statement called SELECT. It can be considered the most important SQL statement for data science simply because its function is to retrieve the data stored in the tables.

It is a very powerful instruction, which allows the specification of different line filtering criteria, can efficiently combine information stored in different tables (an operation known as join), and can even produce simple tabulations.

In the examples presented throughout the chapter, SQLite will be our main working tool - a small library that has direct integration with Python and can "emulate" a relational database management system with great effectiveness.

Database

In a simplified way, we can define database (DB) as a central repository of information that can be consulted and/or updated by several users simultaneously, usually through some application or system. The below figure depicts the setting.

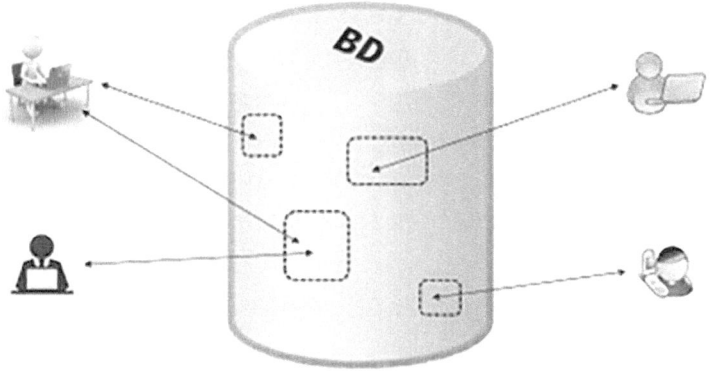

- At the center of the above Figure is the comic book itself: a collection of data managed by a computer called a comic book server. In general, a server is a machine with sophisticated hardware and large storage capacity or consists of a cluster of computers.

- A comic book is almost always a collection of data about the operations and business of a company or organization. These data are produced by the company/organization systems, such as the sales system, HR system, call center service system, academic system (in the case of a university), etc..

- The Figure above also shows several online users who interact with the DB from remote terminals: company network computer, home computer with an Internet browser, mobile phone, etc.

- Note also that some users are simultaneously accessing the same portions of the database (i.e., performing concurrent access to the same data). A practical example of this type of situation occurs, for example, when two or more users of a sales system are referring to the same product.

Database Management Systems (DBMS)

A Database Management System (DBMS) can be defined as special and very sophisticated software that allows the definition, construction, manipulation, and sharing of databases between various users and applications. It is also used to ensure the security of data by protecting it from failure (by example, hardware failures) or unauthorized access attempts.

Although there are different DBMS models, the relational model is the dominant market standard, being adopted by the most used DBMS, such as Oracle, Microsoft SQL Server, PostgreSQL, MySQL, and DB2.

DBMSs represent one of the most developed and reliable software categories among all in which we can classify computer systems. From the '80s on, the use of DBMS began to become common practice in companies, and nowadays, it is rare to find one that does not use this type of software.

They have become so popular that the terms "DBMS" and "database" are often used as synonyms (but it is important to clarify that the concepts are different -

DBMS is actually the software that manages databases, i.e., the databases reside in DBMSs).

SQL

The relational DBMSs are manipulated through a standard language specially developed for the relational environment, called SQL (Structured Query Language). Many researchers in the database area consider it to be the main responsible for the immense popularity achieved by relational DBMSs over the last 30 years.

SQL is offered in virtually all programming environments and is even available in statistical software such as R and SAS. This language is composed of a reduced set of instructions that allow manipulating a comic book with different purposes. The main SQL statements are presented in the table below.

Main SQL statements and their different purposes

Instructions	Purpose	Description
SELECT	Data Recovery	Recovers records stored in database tables.
INSERT DELETE UPDATE	Data Manipulation	Inserting, changing, and removing table records from the database. This subset of SQL statements is known as the *Data Manipulation Language*

		(DML).
CREATE ALTER DROP	Data Definition	Creating, changing, and deleting objects from the database (e.g., tables, indexes, etc.). This subset of instructions is known as DDL (*Data Definition Language*).
COMMIT ROLLBACK	Transaction Control	Manage changes made by HFCK commands. Enables you to group data changes into logical transactions.
GRANT REVOKE	Access Control	Assign or remove access rights to the database and its objects. They are known as DCL (*Data Control Language)* instructions.

The database is an extremely rich and comprehensive subject. So much so that in the undergraduate course in Computer Science, the study of theoretical and practical aspects on database usually occupies two or more disciplines in the grid, such as Database I, Database II, Database Design, NoSQL Databases, and so on. Books adopted by universities usually exceed a thousand pages!

For this reason, we have opted for a much more objective approach in this work. We will focus on a single theme of the comic book universe: the SELECT statement of the SQL language. This instruction is used to retrieve data from tables, allowing the specification of filters, the junction of tables, and even being able to produce aggregations. SELECT is the most commonly used instruction in data analysis processes!

This is because, in the most common scenario, the data scientist will not be authorized to "hack" into the database of a corporate system by creating new tables and changing existing data. Conversely, it will only be given the right (GRANT) to select the data set of interest for the study it wishes to perform. And the only SQL command intended for data selection is exactly our beloved SELECT. End of story!

In the following lessons, we'll show you how to use the SELECT command on small databases created in SQLite (which are part of our book's background material). SQLite was chosen as our working DBMS because it has a lot of interesting features, like:

(i)   is already automatically available for use in Python, not requiring the installation and configuration of any library;

(ii)   supports the SQL language almost in its entirety;

(iii)   generates the databases in single, portable binary files, i.e., you can create a comic book on a Windows computer and then use it on a Linux machine, an iPhone, an Android phone, etc. (a single SQLite file can store up to 2 terabytes of data!).

The standard library's 'sqlite3' library allows Python programs to manipulate BDs created in SQLite using the SQL language. To use it in your programs, perform the import as follows:

```
import sqlite3
```

SQL: Basic SELECT

Introducing the "Company.db" Database

In this lesson, you will learn some examples of basic SELECT command usage. We will work with a small SQLite DB formed by two tables, called "Profession" and "Functional," presented in the below tables.

• The "Occupation" table contains a list of "ids" (codes) and "names" of professions, while "Clerk" stores the "registration," "name," "age," "gender," and "occupation id" of different employees of a company. Thus, "Profession" has two columns, while "Functionary" has five. In

196

DB area jargon, table columns are called attributes.

- The "id" column of "Profession" is used to identify each record (row) in the table uniquely. It is called the primary key of the table. Similarly, the "mat" column is the primary key of "Employee."

- The "id_prof" columns of "Function" and "id" of "Profession" serve as a link attribute between both tables. More specifically, the "id_prof" field of "Employee" is a foreign key referencing the "id" field of "Profession." This means that there is an integrity restriction that states that an employee's profession must respect some of the codes registered in "Profession" or have a NULL value (SQL NULL is basically the same thing as Python None).

Profession

ID	Name
1	Engineer
2	Developer
3	Data Scientist
4	Data Miner
5	Mathematician

Employee

Mat	Name	Age	Sex	Id_Prof
M01	George	58	M	5
M02	Jane	32	F	3
M03	Aldcus	40	M	3
M04	Thomas	28	M	1
M05	Mary	43	F	NULL

The two tables were created in an SQLite database called "RH.db," which is part of our course support material. If you have not yet downloaded the material, please do so, as it will be necessary for the execution of the examples contained in the chapter.

Program 53 - Connect Python to SQLite

This example shows the basic recipe for connecting Python to an SQLite DB and query it via SQL. We use as an example the SQL command to return all rows and columns of the table "Employee":

```
SELECT * FROM Functional
```

As indicated above, to display all columns of a table, you must use the keyword SELECT with an "*" (asterisk). The table to be consulted must be indicated after the keyword FROM.

#

P053 SELECT *

```
import sqlite3


#(1) - Connects with the comic book

nameBD = 'C: /PythonCourse/RH.db'

my_conn = sqlite3.connect(nameBD)


#(2) - Run SQL

c = my_cursor() c.execute('SELECT * FROM
Employee')


#(3) - Display the results


  #(3.1) - Obtains and displays column names
names_columns = next(zip( * c.description))
print(names_columns)


#(3.2) - Obtains and displays each recovered DB
line

for line in c: print(line)
```

#(4) - Close the connection

my_conn.close()

Output[53]:

('mat', 'name', 'age', 'sex', 'id_prof')

('M01', 'George', 58, 'M', 5)

('M02', 'Jane', 32, 'F', 3)

('M03', 'Aldous', 40, 'M', 3)

('M04', 'Thomas', 28, 'M', 1)

('M05', 'Mary', 43, 'F', None)

The following is a detailed explanation of each program line:

- **import** sqlite3

    o Import the "sqlite3" module.

- my_conn   =
  sqlite3.**connect**('C:/CursoPython/RH.db')

    o   Uses the **connect()** function of the
    'sqlite3' module to create a "**connection**"
    to the SQLite database structured in the
    "RH.db" file.

- The name "connection" is used because most of the time - especially if we are using "real" DBMSs like Oracle or SQL Server - the DB will be stored on a database server, which corresponds to a different machine than the one where the Python program is running. However, when we work with SQLite, the DB will usually consist of a local file on the same machine.

- c = my_conn. **cursor()**

  - Uses the **cursor()** function of the 'sqlite3' module to create a *cursor* associated to the connection. A *cursor* is something very similar to a *file handle*, but it will allow us to perform operations on data from a DB instead of a file. Thus, opening a cursor is conceptually similar to opening a text file with the **open()** command.

- c. **execute**('SELECT * FROM Employee')

  - Once the *cursor* is opened, we can execute any SQL statement on the DB using the **execute()** function. In this example, we used the **SELECT** statement *, which will return a result set composed of all the rows and columns in the "Function" table. See that the SQL statement is passed in a string as a parameter to **execute the ()** function.

- names_columns = **next(zip(*c. description))**

- **print**(names_columns)

  ○ Here we are using **description**, a **property** of *cursor-type* objects, to get the column names retrieved by the SQL command. We use a "trick," which involves the use of the **zip()** function to throw the column names into a tuple-type data structure. We will not give a detailed explanation of the **zip()** function, which is not part of the scope of our book. Just use the recipe above and you'll always get the column names of a result you get by executing the SELECT statement.

- **is** line **in** c:

print(line)

  ○ Scans the entire result set sequentially, from the first to the last line. Pretty simple and intuitive, huh? It is important to note that each row returned from the table is stored in a Python **tuple**. This makes perfect sense, since tuples are immutable and, when we work with SELECT, we don't want to change the original DB data, but only get a set of results to analyze in the Python program.

- o Just like when we're scanning a file sequentially, the *cursor* only knows how to "move forward." Once we get past a line in the **for** command, there's no way back to the previous one.

- c = **my_close()conn**.

  - o Closes the connection to the database.

Program 54 - Selection of Specific Columns from a Table

To select specific columns from a table, the names of the columns in question must be separated by commas immediately after the SELECT keyword. The following example shows the command to retrieve only the name and age of employees.

```
#

P054 Selecting Specific Columns from a Table

import sqlite3


 #(1) - Connects with the comic book

nameBD = 'C: /PythonCourse/RH.db'
```

```
my_conn = sqlite3.connect(nameBD)
```

```
#(2) - Run SQL
```

```
c = my_conn.cursor()
```

```
W.run('SELECT      name,      age      FROM
Functionary')#(3)  -  Display  results#(3.1)  -
Obtains   and   displays   column   names
names_columns = next(zip( * c.description))
print(names_columns)
```

```
#(3.2) - Obtains and displays each recovered DB
line
```

25 "Property."

is a concept that belongs to the world of object-oriented programming. It basically consists of a variable used to describe the characteristic of an object.

```
for line in c  print(line)
```

```
#(4) - Close the connection
```

```
my_conn.close()
```

Output[54]:

('name', 'age')

('George', 58)

('Jane', 32)

('Aldous', 40)

('Thomas', 28)

('Mary', 43)

Notice that the program is almost identical to the previous one, having only one change: we changed the SQL string to be executed by the cursor from 'SELECT * FROM Functionary' to 'SELECT name, age FROM Functionary.' In the remaining programs of this lesson, the same thing will always happen. We already have our recipe ready to search for information in the comic book with SELECT!

Program 55 - Restricting the Set of Returned Lines (WHERE)

In this example, we will use a SELECT instruction to retrieve the name and age of employees whose "job id" is 3 (i.e., employees whose profession is "Data Scientist"). To do this, you must use the WHERE clause with condition id_prof = 3.

#

P055 Restricting the set of returned lines(WHERE)

import sqlite3


```
#(1) - Connects with the comic book

nameBD = 'C:/CursoPython/RH.db'

my_conn = sqlite3.connect(nameBD)


#(2) - Run SQL

c = my_conn.cursor()

c.execute('SELECT name, age FROM Function WHERE id_prof=3')#(3) - Display results#(3.1) - Obtains and displays column names names_columns = next(zip( * c.description)) print(names_columns)


#(3.2) - Obtains and displays each recovered DB line

for line in c: print(line)


#(4) - Close the connection
```

my_conn.close()

Output[55]: ('name', 'age')

('Jane', 32)

('Aldous', 40)

In more detail, the SQL statement used in this example requests that the values of the columns "name" and "age" of the table "Function" be recovered considering only the rows where the column "id_prof" has a value equal to 3. Since there are only two lines that meet this condition, only two results are returned in the response assembly.

It is important to note that the WHERE clause supports the definition of complex conditions, concatenated by logical operators (AND, OR, NOT). In other words, how a WHERE condition is mounted is the same as that used for the if command.

Program 56 - Ordering the Results (ORDER BY)

You can specify that the results are sorted by one or more columns using the ORDER BY clause. The following example shows a query that returns employees sorted by age.

#

P056 SELECT with ORDER BY

```python
import sqlite3

#(1) - Connects with the comic book

nameBD = 'C:/CursoPython/RH.db'

my_conn = sqlite3.connect(nameBD)


#(2) - Run SQL

c = my_conn.cursor()

c.execute('SELECT * FROM Functionary
ORDER BY age')#(3) - Display the results#(3.1)
- Obtains and displays column names
names_columns = next(zip( * c.description))
print(names_columns)


#(3.2) - Obtains and displays each recovered DB
line

for line in c: print(line)


#(4) - Close the connection

my_conn.close()
```

Output[56]:

```
('mat', 'name', 'age', 'sex',
'id_prof')
  ('M04', 'Thomas', 28, 'M', 1)
  ('M02', 'Jane', 32, 'F', 3)
  ('M03', 'Aldous', 40, 'M', 3)
  ('M05', 'Mary', 43, 'F', None)
  ('M01', 'George', 58, 'M', 5)
```

SQL: Joining Tables

Joins are used in SELECT statements to retrieve data from two tables and "join" them together to produce a combined output. The tables involved in a junction will need to have a common attribute. In our example, the "id of the profession" is who "connects" the tables "Profession" and "Function," that is, it is the common attribute. Note that SQL does not require the link attribute to have the same name in the two tables that will be combined.

Program 57 - INNER JOIN

The internal junction (INNER JOIN) selects all the lines of both tables as long as there is a coincidence in the values of the columns specified in the junction condition. In the example below, INNER JOIN is used to obtain a list of all employees and the names of their professions.

#

P057 SELECT with INNER JOIN

209

```python
import sqlite3

#(1) - Connects with the comic book
nameBD = 'C:/CursoPython/RH.db'
my_conn = sqlite3.connect(nameBD)

#(2) - Mount and Run SQL
c = my_conn.cursor()

vSQL = ""
"SELECT F.*, P.*

FROM Funcionario F INNER JOIN Profession
P ON(F.id_prof = P.id)
"""
"

c.e xecute(vSQL)

#(3) - Display the results
```

```
#(3.1) - Obtains and displays column names
names_columns = next(zip( * c.description))
print(names_columns)
```

```
#(3.2) - Obtains and displays each recovered DB line
```

```
for line in c: print(line)
```

```
#(4) - Close the connection
```

```
my_conn.close()
```

Output[57]:
```
    ('mat', 'name', 'age', 'sex',
'id_prof', 'id', 'name')
    ('M01', 'George', 58, 'M', 5, 5,
'Mathematician')
    ('M02', 'Jane', 32, 'F', 3, 3, 'Data
scientist')
    ('M03', 'Aldous', 40, 'M', 3, 3, 'Data
scientist')
    ('M04', 'Thomas', 28, 'M', 1, 1,
'Engineer')
```

Before we present the explanation about INNER JOIN itself, let's talk about a small novelty introduced in this program: this time, the SELECT statement was not specified directly in c. execute(), but in a string variable called vSQL:

vSQL = """SELECT F.*, P.*

FROM Employee F INNER JOIN Profession P
ON (F.id_prof = P.id)

"""

We adopted this procedure because this SELECT is "longer" than the previous ones! See that we define it in 3 lines! Actually, to make the string occupy more than one line, it was necessary to open and close it using three quotes: ""." Python works that way.

Now let's talk about INNER JOIN because this is a really important subject. To perform the internal junction between two tables in SQL, just follow the same recipe:

1. Specify the names of the tables involved in joining in the FROM clause. Each table will be able to receive a "nickname," used to simplify the reference to them. In our example, "Employee" received the nickname "F" and "Profession" the nickname "P."

2. Specify the type of INNER JOIN junction between the two tables.

3. To make the junction between the two tables effective, it is necessary to write the keyword ON and then specify in parentheses the junction condition between the two tables. This simply means indicating which attribute "links" the two

tables, i.e., which column is present in the two tables. In this case, it is the "id of the profession," which is called "id" in Profession and is called "id_prof" in Employees.

The final junction was then defined as:

> FROM Funcionario F INNER JOIN Profession P ON (F.id_prof = P.id)

Note that next to the word SELECT, the selected fields are now preceded by the nickname of each table to indicate which table each column belongs to (table "F" or table "P"). Also note that the "M05-Mary" employee does not appear in the final result, because she does not have an associated profession code (she has the NULL value stored in the "id_prof" column).

Program 58 - LEFT JOIN

The LEFT JOIN (or LEFT OUTER JOIN) operation returns all the lines in the table on the left, even if there is no matching (equivalent value) in the table on the right. In our example, the "M05-Mary" employee does not have a registered profession. If we wish to produce a list containing all employees with their respective job names, including employees without a registered profession, we must make use of LEFT JOIN, as shown in the example below:

> #

> P058 SELECT with LEFT JOIN

```python
import sqlite3

#(1) - Connects with the comic book
nameBD = 'C:/CursoPython/RH.db'
my_conn = sqlite3.connect(nameBD)

#(2) - Mount and Run SQL
c = my_conn.cursor()

vSQL = ""
"SELECT F.*, P.*

FROM Functionary F LEFT JOIN Profession P
ON(F.id_prof = P.id)
"""
"

c.execute(vSQL)

#(3) - Display the results
```

```
#(3.1) - Obtains and displays column names
names_columns = next(zip( * c.description))
print(names_columns)
```

```
#(3.2) - Obtains and displays each recovered DB
line
```

```
for line in c: print(line)
```

```
#(4) - Close the connection
```

```
my_conn.close()
```

Output[58]:
```
 ('mat', 'name', 'age', 'sex',
'id_prof', 'id', 'name')
 ('M01', 'George', 58, 'M', 5, 5,
'Mathematician')
 ('M02', 'Jane', 32, 'F', 3, 3, 'Data
scientist')
 ('M03', 'Aldous', 40, 'M', 3, 3, 'Data
scientist')
 ('M04', 'Thomas', 28, 'M', 1, 1,
'Engineer')
 ('M05', 'Mary', 43, 'F', None, None,
None)
```

To perform the LEFT JOIN between two tables in SQL the recipe is the same as the one used for INNER JOIN. The only detail to be changed is that, in the FROM clause, the table which we want to take all the rows to the final result must be specified on the left.

In our example, we wanted all employees in the final result, regardless of whether they had a profession or not, so the table "Employees" was specified on the left of the word LEFT JOIN, while "Profession" was on the right. Regarding the junction condition (ON), the order does not make any difference; that is, it does not matter if you specify "ON (F.id_prof = P.id)" or "ON (P.id = F.id_prof)."

Therefore, to list all positions and employees, even those that do not have an associate employee, we should specify "Occupation" on the left.

SELECT F.*, P.*

FROM Profession P LEFT JOIN Staff F ON (F.id_prof = P.id)

ORDER BY mat;

RIGHT JOIN and FULL JOIN

- SQL also has RIGHT JOIN and FULL JOIN join types. However, none of them are supported by SQLite. The RIGHT JOIN junction returns all the rows of the table on the right, even if there is no matching (equivalent value) in the table on the left. That is, LEFT JOIN and RIGHT JOIN work the same way, and the only difference is that in the first case, we will

216

specify the table to which we want all the lines in the result on the left and in the second case it will be on the right. In practice, the LEFT JOIN has become more adopted by programmers who work with SQL.

- The FULL JOIN joint returns all table rows to the left and all table rows to the right duly combined according to the joint condition specification. If there are lines in the left table that do not match the right table, they are taken to the final result. And if there are rows in the right table that do not have equivalence in the left table, they are also taken to the final result. We will show an example of a FULL JOIN operation in the next book, which will cover the 'pandas' library.

SQL: Producing Aggregate Results

The SELECT statement supports complex queries not only with the use of joins but also with functions for producing aggregated results. Consider aggregation as a data transformation process that produces scalar values from tables, usually using a mathematical or statistical function (sum, average, etc.).

The functions for the production of aggregated results will be presented from examples that explore the table "Project," stored in the SQLite DB called "Reforms.db", whose structure and content are presented in Figure 18.

Project

Code	Type	Place	Cost
P1	A	NJ	500.000
P2	A	NY	900.000
P3	B	NJ	150.000
P4	A	NY	1,000.000
P5	B	CO	NULL
P6	A	NJ	850.000

Consider that this table stores the projects currently conducted by a building renovation company. It has four columns: "code" (project code), type ('A'=Structural Reform or 'B'=Facade Maintenance), "local" (UF where work is being carried out) and "cost" (work budget in $). Note that the project 'P5' does not yet have the budget defined (it has a NULL value stored in the "cost" variable).

Program 59 - COUNT

The COUNT(v) function of the SQL language determines the number of occurrences of non-null values of a given column in a table. On the other hand, COUNT(*) is used to count the total number of rows in a table (instead of counting the number of rows where a specific column has no null value):

```
#

P059 SELECT with COUNT

import sqlite3


  #(1) - Connects with the comic book

nameBD = 'C:/CoursePython/Reforms.db'

my_conn = sqlite3.connect(nameBD)


#(2) - Runs SQL and displays results

c = my_conn.cursor()

vSQL = "SELECT COUNT(code),
COUNT(cost), COUNT(*) FROM Project"

c.execute(vSQL)


for line in c: print(line)


#(3) - Close the connection

my_conn.close()
```

Output[59]:

```
      (6, 5, 6)
```

The first value 6 indicates that this is the number of registers where the "code" variable has no NULL value. Similarly, value 5 indicates that there are five records in which the "cost" variable is not zero. Finally, the last 6 comes from COUNT(*), indicating the number of lines in the "Design" table. Note that in this example, we do not capture and display the column names of the result set (we show only the results).

Program 60 - MAX, MIN, AVG, SUM

For a given column of a table, the MIN, MAX, and AVG functions return, respectively, the minimum, maximum, and average value of the table. The SUM function returns the sum of the column values in all rows. These functions ignore NULL values.

```
#

P060 SELECT with MAX, MIN, AVG, SUM

import sqlite3


#(1) - Connects with the comic book

nameBD = 'C:/CursoPython/Reforms.db'

my_conn = sqlite3.connect(nameBD)


#(2) - Runs SQL and displays results
```

```
c = my_conn.cursor()

vSQL = "SELECT MIN(cost), MAX(cost),
AVG(cost), SUM(cost) FROM Project"

c.execute(vSQL)

for line in c: print(line)


#(3) - Close the connection

my_conn.close()
```
Output[60]:
```
(150000, 1000000, 680000.0, 3400000)
```

Program 61 - GROUP BY

The GROUP BY clause can be combined with group functions to enable the production of aggregated results by one or more columns. The example below gives the minimum, maximum, average, and sum of the cost per project type.

```
#

P061 SELECT with GROUP BY

import sqlite3


#(1) - Connects with the comic book
```

```
nameBD = 'C:/CursoPython/Reforms.db'

my_conn = sqlite3.connect(nameBD)


#(2) - Runs SQL and displays results

c = my_conn.cursor() vSQL = ""
"

SELECT

type,  MIN(cost),  MAX(cost),  AVG(cost),
SUM(cost)


FROM Project GROUP BY type ""
"


c.execute(vSQL)

for line in c: print(line)


#(3) - Close the connection

my_conn.close()
```

Output[61]:

```
    ('A', 500000, 1000000, 812500.0,
3250000)
    ('B', 150000, 150000, 150000.0,
150000)
```

Program 62 - HAVING

If you want to delete a group from the final result produced by a SELECT with GROUP BY, it is necessary to use the HAVING clause. In the example below, all groups in which the sum of the costs is less than 600,000 are deleted.

```
#

P062 SELECT with GROUP BY and HAVING

import sqlite3


  #(1) - Connects with the comic book

nameBD = 'C:/CursoPython/Reforms.db'

my_conn = sqlite3.connect(nameBD)


#(2) - Runs SQL and displays results

c = my_conn.cursor() vSQL = ""

"
```

```
SELECT

type, site, SUM(cost)

FROM Project

GROUP BY type, location

HAVING SUM(cost) >= 600000 ""

"
```

c.e xecute(√SQL)

for line in c: print(line)

#(3) - Close the connection

my_conn.close()

Output[62]:
```
('A', 'DF', 1900000)
('A', 'SP', 850000)
```

That brings us to the end of the chapter and to the nearest to the conclusion of this book. We gave a brief introduction to the SQL language focusing on the most common uses of SELECT intrusion in data science programs. As with regular expressions, SQL language is a theme that, in itself, requires an entire book to be presented in detail.

Conclusion

We have made our hands dirty on Data Science with Python in this book, and now we need to delve a little deeper into the concepts related to data analysis before continuing on Python's advantages over other languages. Throughout the history of civilization, the data we had was mostly structured and small in size and could be analyzed with simple tools. Unlike data in traditional systems, which were mostly structured, today, most data is unstructured or semi-structured.

Estimates indicate that by 2020, over 80% of the data will be unstructured. This data is generated from diverse sources such as financial records, forms, text files, sensors, and various instruments. Simple tools cannot handle this huge variety and volume of data. That's why we need more complex solutions and advanced analytical algorithms to process, analyze, and extract significant insights.

However, this is not the only reason Data Science has become so popular and relevant. And if you could understand exactly what your customers need from their existing data, such as browsing history, purchase history, age, and income, you would undoubtedly have all that data before. But you can now train the models much more efficiently and recommend the product to your clientele more accurately from the wealth and variety of information available. Amazing, right?

Let's imagine a futuristic scenario for understanding Data Science's role in decision making. What if your car had the intellect to drive you to the home? Autonomous cars collect live data from radars, cameras, sensors, and lasers to generate a map of the surroundings. Combining this data, it makes decisions about when to accelerate, when to slow down, the perfect time for overtaking, and turning points, using radical ML 9Machine Learning) algorithms.

We can also use Data Science in PA Models (Predictive Analytics Models). Let's take the weather forecast as an example. Data from aircraft, radars, ships, and satellites can be gathered and analyzed to create models. These models not only predict the climate but also help to predict the incidence of any natural disasters. This will help you take appropriate action beforehand and save lives.

This book introduced the basics of Python programming. It covered only those topics considered relevant to those who wish to work with Python in data science, starting with the elementary aspects of the language - variables, data structures, deviation and repetition statements, and function creation, going through the processing of strings and text files, ending with an introduction to the SQL language.

As this is an introductory book, several important issues could not be addressed. Below is a list of topics that will be covered broadly for those who wish to continue their studies to become advanced pythonists:

- Standard Python: Since this book failed to address some topics considered a little more "dense" than standard Python. An example: creating lambda expressions and combining them with map() and reduce() functions.

- Configuring the Python environment: package management and the creation of virtual environments represent two advanced but important themes for those who want to use Python professionally.

- pandas: In next book of Data Science With Python Series, we will present an overview of the 'pandas' library, focusing mainly on importing different file types and performing basic operations (indexing, slicing, creating/removing columns, filtering rows, generating aggregates, joining and concatenating DataFrames). However, this library is very sophisticated and offers a huge set of tools for cleaning and data transformation. To be honest, it would take at least another 200 pages to cover all the features of the 'pandas'! Therefore, we consider it important that you study and learn more about the library to work on professional data science projects.

- Jupyter Notebook: is a web application for the creation of notebooks, which basically consists of data science projects developed using Python, R, or other technologies. Jupyter Notebook is similar to a programming IDE, but it is much better! This is because a notebook can store both the source code (the program itself), as well as the databases used and the results obtained in a certain process of data analysis (graphics, tables, reports, models, etc.). Even better, notebooks can be published on the Web and shared with other users in a simple and fast way. For these reasons, Jupyter Notebook has become one of the most popular applications for data science.

- Scikit-learn: a library that contains the implementation of various algorithms for data mining and machine learning (algorithms for classification, cluster analysis, regression, attribute selection, etc.).

- Scipy: a library that offers efficient numerical routines for integration and optimization.

- Keras, FastAI, TensorFlow, and PyTorch: these libraries are especially recommended for those who wish to work with neural networks and deep learning.

- NLTK (Natural Language Toolkit): set of libraries for text mining and natural language processing.

- Web Scraping: The standard Python language is endowed with excellent resources for those who wish to work with Web scraping. In addition to the great functions for string handling and the 're' module (regular expressions), the standard library itself offers the 'socket' module for HTTP connection and data recovery from web pages. And outside the standard library, there are also much more powerful packages for Web scraping, such as Scrapy and Beautiful Soup.

- XML: This is an information representation scheme that can be considered "rival" to JSON. In Python, XML files can be processed, among other ways, through the 'xml' module of the standard library.

- Object Orientation in Python: Although the procedural paradigm is best suited for developing scripts for data science, it is important to make it clear that the object-oriented aspects of Python are very useful in many practical situations. Therefore, they also deserve to receive attention from aspiring professional pythonists.

Finally, A Very Big Hug to The World of Data Science With Python!